The MINNESOTA ROAD GUIDE To GANGSTER HOT SPOTS

D1542185

By Chad Lewis

THE MINNESOTA ROAD GUIDE TO GANGSTER HOT SPOTS

The Minnesota Road Guide To Gangster Hotspots
Copyright 2009
ISBN: 978-0-9824314-0-5
The Road Publications
www.OnTheRoadPublications.com

Chad Lewis
of
On The Road Publications

Author Chad Lewis
Design Chad Lewis and Noah Voss
Layout Noah Voss
Editor Sarah Szymanski

ACKNOWLEDGMENTS

I would like to thank Nisa Giaquinto, Noah Voss, and Sarah Szymanski for assisting me with the research and production of the book.

I would also like to thank the numerous historical societies, librarians, and researchers, who provided extensive research for this book. I would like to give a special thanks to those who took the time and effort to share their memories with me about the crimes that impacted their families and communities.

Dedication

This book is dedicated to the Giaquinto Family of Winona, Minnesota whose liveliness could rival any 1930's soiree.

The Minnesota Road Guide To Gangster Hot Spots

Table Of Contents

The Minnesota Road Guide To Gangster Hot Spots

Table Of Contents

INTRODUCTION

"My claim to fame is that I got a sock in the jaw from 'Baby Face' Nelson."
- Bank Employee Zane Smith

First of all this book is simply about adventure! Whether you just have a passing interest in gangsters or you have a set of Tommy Guns in your trunk, this guide is set up for you to enjoy. Filled with directions, photos, newspaper accounts, and eyewitness reports, this book provides you with everything you need to explore Minnesota's gangster past. It is your decision whether you want to enjoy this book from the comfort of your favorite reading chair, or if you want to retrace the steps of the infamous gangsters by visiting each location for yourself. Either way, you will be whisked away on a journey around the state to places where gangsters robbed banks, had shoot-outs with the authorities, bribed police, murdered each other, kidnapped wealthy citizens, and danced the night away.

There is no better place to explore gangster history than in Minnesota. While the media created the fantasy that gangsters never left Chicago, the truth is that Minnesota was truly ground zero for criminals. No other place in the country provided the gangsters with so many opportunities to further their criminal aspirations. If you needed police protection from the law, you found it in Minnesota. If you were looking to rob a bank and needed an extra man, you found it in Minnesota. If you needed to launder stolen bank bonds, you found it in Minnesota. If you wanted to upgrade your arsenal…well you get the idea. This system of catering to gangsters was so successful that nearly every big name gangster of the day ended up spending some time in Minnesota.

Here is where the adventure aspect of this book comes into play because fortunately for you many of these gangster hot spots are still standing today. Although some locations have been renovated, some have changed businesses, and some are nearly unrecognizable, the important history of these buildings still remain. And while infamous gangsters no longer reside in Minnesota (excluding politicians), the locations where these men and women created history still do.

Keep an eye out,
Chad Lewis

Robbers
Strike Bank

Shoot-Out

Wanted

ROGUES
GALLERY

REWARD

Murder!

Kidnapping

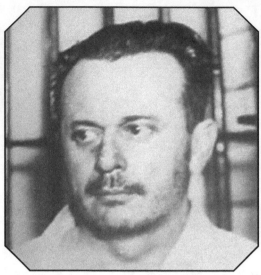

Arthur "Doc" Barker- Doc was born in Missouri in 1899. From an early age Barker was in and out of prison and was best known for teaming up with his brother Fred Barker, and fellow gangster Alvin "Creepy" Karpis. Doc was eventually sentenced to Alcatraz where he was killed while attempting to escape.

Fred Barker- Was described by many as a cold-blooded killer. Barker formed the Barker-Karpis gang with his brother Doc Barker, and Alvin Karpis. Fred met his end when he and his mother were shot to death during a 1935 raid on their Florida rental cabin.

Ma Barker- Ma Barker was born Arizona Donnie Clark in Missouri. She was portrayed as the outlaw mother of the Barker boys. After being killed in a shootout in Florida, the FBI fabricated the legend of the woman, who it was said could not plan breakfast, much less a bank robbery. Ma Barker was killed in 1935 alongside her son Fred in a shootout at their Florida rental cabin.

George "Machine Gun" Kelly Barnes- Originally from Tennessee, Kelly quickly became one of the nation's best known criminals. The famous moniker of "Machine Gun Kelly" was given to him by his wife, Kathryn Thorne, who was believed by many to be the driving force behind his life of crime. In 1954, on his 59th birthday, Kelly suffered a heart attack and died while still

serving time in Leavenworth Prison.

Tommy Carroll- Born in Montana, Carroll was a Chicago area bank robber who worked closely with John Dillinger, Baby Face Nelson, and Homer Van Meter. Carroll was killed by two detectives in Waterloo, Iowa in 1934.

John Paul Chase- Chase lived a mostly straight life in California, until he accepted a job as an armed guard for a truck smuggling illegal liquor. Chase's co-worker on the job was George "Baby Face" Nelson. While working together, the two men became fast friends. In 1934, after the death of Baby Face, Chase was eventually arrested and sentenced to Alcatraz Prison. Over the years, Chase was transferred to several prisons until his final release in 1966. In 1973, Chase succumbed to cancer and died in California.

Larry "The Chopper" Devol- Devol was a bank robber who often joined up with the Barker-Karpis gang robbing banks and kidnapping wealthy businessmen. In 1936, Devol was killed in a shootout with police in Enid, Oklahoma.

John Dillinger- Born in Indiana in 1903, John Dillinger went on to become the nation's most famous bank robber during the 1930s. Dillinger was considered Public Enemy #1 when he was gunned down outside Chicago's Biograph Theater in 1934.

Evelyn "Billie" Frechette – A Wisconsin native, Billie was best known for being the girlfriend of John Dillinger. Once captured, Billie served two years in prison for harboring her boyfriend. After prison Billie lived a quiet life in Wisconsin until her death in 1969.

Leon Gleckman- Gleckman was considered the Al Capone of St. Paul. A bootlegger with considerable political ties, Gleckman controlled much of the crime in St. Paul.

Fred Goetz.

Fred Goetz- Aka- "Shotgun George" Ziegler- Goetz was a henchman for Al Capone in Chicago and was one of the alleged shooters in the St. Valentine's Day Massacre. Goetz also participated in the St. Paul kidnapping. In 1934, Goetz was killed in Chicago during a drive-by shooting.

John Hamilton- Aka- Red, Three Finger Jack - Hamilton met John Dillinger while the two of them were severing time in prison together. After prison Hamilton went on a crime spree with Dillinger and was killed in Hastings, MN during a car chase with authorities.

"Dapper" Dan Hogan-
Hogan was the owner of St. Paul's notorious Green Lantern Saloon. Hogan seemed to have his hand in the majority of the crimes committed in the Twin Cities. Hogan was killed in 1928 when a car bomb went off when he tried to start his car.

Alvin "Old Creepy" Karpis-

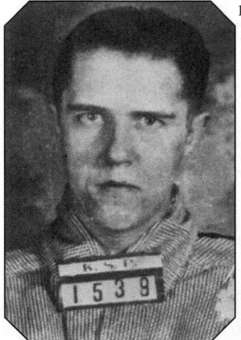

Karpis, who was born Alvin Karpowicz, was best known for joining forces with the Barker gang. Karpis was considered one of the smartest gangsters of his time. Karpis was finally captured in 1936, and sent to Alcatraz Prison where he spent more time than any other inmate before being paroled in 1969. Karpis died in 1979 from a pill overdose.

Dr. Clayton May- Dr. May ran an illegal clinic performing abortions and treating unsavory clients. Dr. May was sentenced to two years in prison for his role in aiding John Dillinger, who came to him with a bullet wound in his leg.

Verne Miller- As a former police officer and sheriff, Miller started out on the right side of the law. Having found law enforcement not to his liking, Miller sought the excitement that a life of crime provided. Miller is best known as being one of the men responsible for the Kansas City Massacre of 1933, which took the life of fellow gangster Frank Nash, and four law enforcement agents. Not long after the massacre, Miller's lifeless body was discovered in a ditch outside of Detroit.

George "Baby Face" Nelson- Real Name Lester Gillis. Baby Face was born in Chicago in 1908, and was on the wrong side of the law from an early age. Mostly considered a hotheaded killer, Nelson was perhaps the best connected gangster in the Midwest. Often Nelson was the one to secure safe houses, weapons, cars, and unsavory business associates for his colleagues. During his legacy of crime and murder, Nelson was married with two children, and was described as a devoted husband. In 1934, Nelson died in a shoot out with the law just outside of Chicago.

John J. O'Connor – The corrupt police chief that is credited with allowing gangsters to freely roam St. Paul as long as they stayed out of trouble and paid a percentage of their earnings to the department.

John J. O'Connor
Chief of Police

Jack Peifer- Peifer was the proprietor of the Hollyhocks Inn where he paid off police and served as an underworld banker. Peifer was sentenced to prison for his role in the kidnappings of William Hamm and Edward Bremer. In 1936, while waiting to be sent to prison, Peifer committed suicide in his cell by taking a cyanide pill.

Harry "Dutch" Sawyer- Sawyer was a bootlegger best known for working at the Green Lantern for "Dapper" Dan Hogan.

Sawyer was rumored to be the main suspect behind the car-bombing that took his boss' life. After Hogan was murdered, Sawyer took over operations of the Green Lantern, which included many underworld dealings. In 1935, Sawyer was arrested and went on trial for his involvement in the Edward Bremer kidnapping case. After being found guilty, Sawyer was sentenced to prison. In 1955, while suffering from several dire medical conditions, Sawyer was released from prison and died several months later.

Sammy Silverman- Silverman, wanted in Kansas City in con-

nection with several murders, was a well-known gunman and racketeer around Minneapolis. Silverman was thought to be involved in the bank robbery that took place in Willmar, Minnesota. Shortly after the Willmar bank hold-up Silverman's bloody body was discovered near a wooded area in the small town of Mahtomedi, MN.

Homer Van Meter- Van Meter was an associate of both Baby Face Nelson and John Dillinger, who he met while serving time in prison. Newspapers of the 1930s claimed that Van Meter was Dillinger's Lieutenant. Van Meter was shot to death in an alley in St. Paul.

YMCA was a lookout place and suspicioning the office in Murphy's store was also one, machine guns were turned on them to keep everyone out of sight and from any likelihood of pursuit.

Announcement was made over WCCO immediately and local officers also were notified but the birds had fled.

Clues are being followed by operatives of the Bureau of Criminal Apprehension as well as Sheriff Little's office but nothing definite of any kind has as yet developed.

That the gang was here at least ten days is evidenced by one of the bandits who said that to his knowledge he had opened t h e bank door each m o r n i n g for 10 days when George begged that he had no key to open the door.

The bandits wore masks part of the time at _____ only and a good desc_____tion o_____ber is known.

Dorothy Kinne ___nd R_____ derson passed i_____ the bank just as the shooting started.

President George D. LaBar and vice president Fred Farrar and auditi__ _enry ___e did not arrive __ after ba___, its had left.

It is extre____ __ tu____ __ no one wa____kill__ w____ bandits opened fire. The bank loss is entirely covered by insurance.

+ Pio n e e r settlers who had g o o d lake sites were often forced to accommodate o v e r night guests who came to hunt and fish.

FIRST NATIONAL BANK—The above picture shows the First National Bank in about 1920 at its longtime location at Sixth and Front. Below is a picture of the same building as it looked many years earlier before the building was remodeled. The bank now is in new quarters at Maple and Sixth.

BRAINERD
MINNESOTA

NORTHERN PACIFIC BANK—This is the interior of the Northern Pacific Bank as it looked in the 1890s. The bank was organized in November, 1889. The Northern Pacific Bank became the Citizens State Bank in 1906.

+ There were 200 s u m m e r resorts in the Brainerd lake region in 1940.

+ A trading post usually consisted of shop, clerk's house, house for men, a clearing for potatoes and corn surrounded by high stockade built of 12 logs set on end in holes dug into the ground, often a roof house, flag staff and well.

+ Father Pierz records that traders did all possible to retard and place obstacles in the way of missionaries. The reason was to retard training of Indians in agriculture thus keeping the Indians at hunting and trapping for livlihood.

+ In 1872, Brainerd was a wild and wooly town — all early writings make reference to this point.

+ There were several routes used by the Indians to reach the Mississippi River from Mille Lacs Lake and thus to north, south and east points.

+ Indians were determined to stop progress — they stretched a rope of moose skin across the tracks near Deerwood in an effort to stop the first train. They w e r e unsuccessful and were sent tumbling into snowbanks. They made no further efforts to stop trains.

11

Robbery of the First National Bank

Location:

201 S 6th St.

Brainerd, MN 56401

(218) 828-3693

Currently: T&B Pawn Shop

Directions:

Take Highway 210 (Washington St.) to the east and turn right onto S 6th St. The old bank building will be on your left and the original bank etching can be seen on the top of the building.

Gangster Lore:

The money that regular everyday citizens deposited and invested with the First National Bank in Brainerd was insured by the Federal Government. This comforting fact made the residents around the county a little more ambivalent about their banks being robbed. During the depression many banks foreclosed on family farms, leading to the widespread public perception that the banks were the real bad guys. The gangsters were merely robbing the banks, who had stolen from the people. However, the people of Brainerd were more upset with the style of the bank robbery, than the robbery itself. The gangsters could have easily exited the city without any ruckus, but instead they decided to shoot up the entire downtown as they hurried away with their loot.

History:

1879 – The first bank in Brainerd was established when William Ferris started a private bank which was aptly called the "Bank of Brainerd."

1881 – Following in the footsteps of the Bank of Brainerd, the First National Bank was established. Its original stock was valued at $50,000. Two of the original members were Judge George W. Holland and Adam Brown.

1882 – The bank held its first annual stockholders meeting to discuss the future of the business and the growth of the town.

1906 – The bank was thriving as evidenced by a deposit statement from the close of business on May 14th that showed a bank balance of $958,688.

1916 – With its growing success the bank purchased the building it had been occupying and began a major renovation of the large brick building.

1929 – The board of directors voted in favor of becoming a charter member of the U.S. banking system, thus providing the security that would calm the nerves of prospective customers.

1933 – The bank was robbed by Baby Face Nelson, Tommy Carroll, Homer Van Meter, John Paul Chase, and Charles Fisher.

1948 – Bank employee Zane Smith received a call stating that his wife had been kidnapped and that he needed to come up with $10,000 in order to secure her safe return. Immediately the authorities were called in, and while the ransom money was being put together Smith drove home to find his wife safe and sound, and the "kidnappers" were never heard from again.

1990s – The bank had been closed down and a Sears store operated in the building.

1999 – T&B Pawn Shop moved into the bank's old building.

Source: Brainerd Dispatch

Investigation:
On October 22 1933, five heavily armed men carrying machine

guns pulled off a daring robbery of the First National Bank. Although the exact members of the robbery were never officially discovered, it is widely believed that the bank heist was pulled off by Baby Face Nelson, Tommy Carroll, John Paul Chase, Homer Van Meter and Charles Fisher. The *Crosby Courier* wrote that Nelson, Van Meter, and Carroll were all identified as the robbers by several Brainerd residents and witnesses. Although the complete identities of the robbers were initially unknown, it was quite clear that they were all experienced crooks. The authorities investigating the case told the media that it was beyond question that the gang was made up of professional bank robbers.

Always looking to cover every conceivable angle of their crime the gang had spent over 10 days casing the Brainerd bank. Their diligent homework paid off at 5:55 am when the bank custodian, George Fricker, showed up to begin his daily routine. Fricker was quickly greeted by a pistol to his ribs and ordered to open up the front doors. According to the *Brainerd Daily Dispatch* the custodian tried to fib his way out of the situation when he told the man that he didn't have a key to open the bank. Pushing his gun a little harder against the bluffing custodian, the gunman said, "the hell you haven't, you've been opening it for the last ten days." With the discovery of his lie, Fricker wisely unlocked the front door. Once inside, the custodian was brought to a back room and instructed to sit quietly on the floor. The next people to enter were Mr. and Mrs. Peterson, the cleaners, who were told to go about their normal routine in order to avoid arousing unwanted suspicion. An hour and a half later Robert Titus, who was the bank's guard, entered the building. In their book *Baby Face Nelson*, Steven Nickel and William Helmer wrote that the guard was at ease because he had seen the cleaning lady going about her duties as usual. Over the next two hours several other employees entered the bank and were secured without any hassle or commotion. This calmness was shattered with the arrival of Zane Smith, the 17-year-old collection clerk. When Zane casually entered the bank he was quickly introduced to the volatile behavior of Baby Face Nelson. Out of nowhere Zane was immediately punched in the jaw by Baby Face, who then dragged the stunned young man along the floor to the back room. The punch seemed a little excessive for a robbery that was going so smoothly, but then again subtly was never Nelson's trademark. Although not amused at the time, years later Zane would tell the *Brainerd Daily Dispatch*, "My claim to fame is that I got a sock in the jaw from 'Baby Face' Nelson." Meanwhile, witnesses outside of the bank no-

ticed an odd man standing near the front doors. Dressed in hunting attire, the out-of –place man was just standing on the corner with a pic-

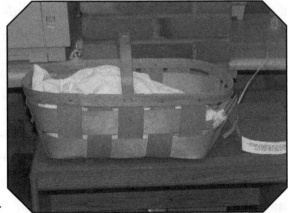

nic basket in his arms. The basket was meant to serve as a ruse to conceal the loaded machine gun that was hiding under a piece of old flour sack.   Once all the key employees had arrived and were properly secured, the gang waited until the time-locked vault could be opened. With everything in control, the gang quickly cleaned the bank out of an estimated $32,000. At approximately 9 a.m. the dozen employees were hauled into the men's room where they were instructed to wait. The *Brainerd Daily Dispatch* quoted an employee who said that Nelson told the crowd, "We're leaving now but anyone who sticks his head out of the door will get his head blown off." Fortunately the group complied with the instructions, as this was a threat that Baby Face was more than capable of delivering on.

Amazingly not one gunshot was fired during the robbery, and the gang exited the bank without any obstacles. Filled with the bank's money the crew piled into a large sedan that they had previously stolen from North Dakota. With a clean getaway in sight the gang sped down the road spraying the downtown buildings and surrounding area with machine gun fire. Authorities estimated that somewhere between 75 and 100 bullets were unnecessarily fired. Luckily no innocent bystanders were hit by the whizzing lead. However, the nearby buildings and business windows were not so lucky, as even today if you look at the First National Bank plaque you can see where a few of the stray bullets hit. The gun fire also caught the attention of police, who up until this point had been oblivious to the robbery. Immediately an extensive manhunt was organized to search surrounding cabins, roads, hideouts, resorts, and anywhere else a fugitive could hide. Authorities even looked into the remote possibility that the gang had used an airplane to escape the area, a far-fetched theory that was quickly dropped. But despite an unrelenting search for the criminals, no one was ever charged with the Brainerd robbery.

THE BRAINERD DAILY DISPATCH

DARING MACHINE GUN MOB ROBS FIRST NATIONAL HERE

IOWA GOVERNOR CALLS FOR EARLY CONFAB ON FARM STRIKE ISSUES

ROBBERY OF FIRST NAT'NAL BANK FIRST IN HISTORY OF CITY; OTHER TOWNS AREA ROBBED RECENT YEARS

Escape After Firing Barrage Machine Gun Bullets Into Place

CUFFS ON JAW, BLOW WITH BUTT END OF REVOLVER AND PUMMELING WITH GUNS IN BACK FELT BY 3 EMPLOYES

FLAT DECLARATION BY F. D. FOR 'SOUND MONEY' SPURS OPTIMISM

F. D. SIGNS RETAIL CODE, EXEMPTS SMALL STORE MAN

Tommy Gun Adventures:

Take a short stroll over to the Crow Wing Historical Society Museum at 320 Laurel Street, where they have the original picnic basket and flour sack that were used to conceal a machine gun during the robbery. The basket may not be out on display, so just like using a speakeasy password, you may have to ask to see it.

CAMBRIDGE
MINNESOTA

MAIN STREET LOOKING SOUTH, CAMBRIDGE, MINN.

The Barker-Karpis Gang Holds the Town Hostage

Location:

Downtown Main Street

Cambridge, MN

Directions:

This case has several places for you to retrace the gangsters'
footsteps. All of the places that the Barker-Karpis gang robbed
are on Main Street in downtown Cambridge. The two hostages
were released near the town of Soderville, and walked to the filling station at Coopers Corner.

Places they robbed:

Gillespie Garage – Now Doctor Mont's Auto

115 Main St. North

Jack Lewis Store — Now Ace Tack & Outfitters, Inc.

103 Main St. South

Fairway Super Market – Now Ace Tack & Outfitters, Inc.

103 Main St. South

Ruyan Drug Store – Now Synergy Sports Store

113 Main St. South

Coopers Corner – Where hostages were dropped off – Now St. Andrew Lutheran Church. Coopers Corner is now part of the town of East Bethel. The location of the filling station is on the southeast corner of Highway 65 and 237th St. NE where the church currently rests.

Gangster Lore:

The motive behind why the Barker-Karpis gang picked Cambridge, Minnesota as the location of their crime spree remains unknown. Perhaps it was due to the fact that the small sleepy town of Cambridge was the last place you would expect armed bandits to rob. Maybe it was the town's relative proximity to the Twin Cities that appealed to the gang. Surely the lack of a large police presence would have also tempted the gangsters. Whatever the reason, with kidnappings, stealing cars, and breaking safes, the gang got a taste of much bigger crimes to come.

History:

Gillespie Garage:

1912 – E.F. Gillespie started selling automobiles to the expanding town.

1920 – The Gillespie Garage was constructed for repairs and storage of vehicles.

1924-25 – Gillespie purchased other garages in Pine City and Mora.

1928 – E.F. Gillespie passed away.

1932 – The garage was robbed by the Barker-Karpis gang. The gang drove out several cars before deciding on a Buick.

1960s – The Gillespie garage was sold to Iten Chevrolet and became Pete Iten's Auto Center.

2000 – Doctor Monte's Auto moved into the building.

Currently – Doctor Monte's Auto resides in the building.

Jack Lewis Store:

1913 – Thieves broke into the store and were unable to open the cash register so they took it with them. The register was found in the back of the building by the horse parking sheds.

1932 – The Barker-Karpis gang broke into the store. The gang took as much merchandise as they could while securing cash from the safe.

Currently – The building houses the Ace Tack & Outfitters.

Fairway Super Market:

1925 – E.F. Gillespie sold the market to Russell Elofson who then changed the name of the store to Elofson's Fairway Market.

1957 – The store was purchased by Robert Nelson.

1960 – The store owners announced that they would be moving to a new location across the street.

1994 – The tack store moved into the building.

Currently – The building houses the Ace Tack & Outfitters.

Runyan Drug Store:

1930s – Guy Runyan opened Runyan Drug.

1932 – The drug store was robbed by the Barker-Karpis gang.

1935 – Donald Anderson had been managing the drug store for many years. When Runyan passed away Anderson purchased the store, and changed the name to Anderson Drug.

1961 – Charlie Phillips joined the Anderson Drug Store crew.

1970s – Charlie Phillips and Jim Barrett took over the store from Anderson.

1998 – The building and business was both sold and the building remained empty.

2008 – The Synergy Sports Store moved into the building.

Currently – The Synergy Sports Store occupies the building.

Investigation:

Around 3 a.m. on January 5, 1932, the Barker-Karpis gang broke into the back of the Gillespie Garage. The noise of the breaking glass had awoken Mart Dunning, the garage attendant, who had been sleeping in his room in the south part of the building. Dun-

ning and his watch dog got up and went to investigate the noise. When he entered the main room he was met by two of the gangsters who ordered him to call off the dog. To help gain his assistance Dunning was struck on the top of the head with the butt end of a gun. Now a bit stunned, Dunning was placed in a chair and guarded by the armed gang. With Dunning being held prisoner, the Barker gang tried to crack open the garage's safe.

After several failed attempts on the safe, the gang had to settle for the measly $25 they retrieved from the cash register. Once all the money was cleaned out, the gang decided they needed a new getaway car. The *Albert Lea Evening Tribune* wrote, "Flaunting sawed-off shotguns and pistols the invaders dared possible apprehension by making practice drives in several automobiles in the garage before selecting one best suited to their purposes." In actuality the gang wasn't joyriding the cars, they were simply moving several of the older cars in order to reach the Buick that they had selected to be taken.

Night Patrolman Frank Whitney was making his routine rounds down the sidewalk when he was caught off guard by the ever watchful gang. Whitney was ordered to put up his hands, and when he complied, the gang quickly removed him of his gun. Being the hardened criminals that they were, the gang even stripped Whitney of the $50 in cash he was carrying that night. Whitney was brought up to the Runyan Drug Company, where inside, the gang was busy gathering up both money and inventory. The gang ransacked the prescription department in search of narcotics, but failed to retrieve any drugs. Whitney recalled the incident in The *North Star* newspaper stating "When they came out of the drug store they walked down to Jack Lewis' side door, the north door. There they stopped me. Mart Dunning was with us. There they batted the door with a sledge hammer. There were three or four fellows there. The others were off with a gun somewhere running around. When they hit, the burglar alarm went off. I heard that. I heard one say to the others 'Oh, *** let's get out of here. It will have the whole town up.' The other said, 'The *** with the town, we aren't going.'" The gang managed to locate a stepladder that they used to unplug the alarm and cut the wires. The helpless hostages watched as the men left the store carrying sacks of coats and dresses along with about eighty-five dollars in cash.

The next stop for the gangsters was the Fairway Market. Fearing that another night guard might be sleeping inside the store, the gang shoved Whitney through the door first. When the store was found to be unoccupied, the gang immediately began attacking the safe. Several heavy hits from the sledge hammer failed to open the safe. When several other crime methods failed to open the safe, the gang grew discouraged and finally gave up. The $30 found in the cash register served as a small consolation prize. By now, nearly one hour had passed since the gang had first broken into the garage, and as they hurriedly loaded their cars with all of the stolen merchandise and cash their attention turned to the hostages. Not willing to take any chance of being caught, the gangsters forced the two men into their vehicles. The *Minneapolis Journal* wrote, "The marshal was forced into a back seat of one of the cars and ordered to lie down on a pile of merchandise." They picked up Dunning and sped out of town on highway No. 5 (Highway 65) toward the Twin Cities. As the miles sped by, the hostages had to have believed that this would be their last night on earth. Although the hostages knew nothing of the cold-blooded killers around them, it surely must have dawned on them that these men were no saints. As they braced for the worst, Dunning and Whitney were safely released approximately 20 miles outside of Cambridge near the town of Soderville. The *Oshkosh Daily Northwestern* reported that Whitney and Dunning had to walk for nearly two hours before they reached a telephone at the filling station at Coopers Corners. The *Billings Gazette* wrote, "There the marshal spread the alarm. The state bureau of criminal apprehension was notified. Radio broad-

UESDAY, JANUARY 5, 1932.   Price Two Cents in Minneap.

JNDER CAMBRIDGE

r on *Changing Pleas* LOOT 4 STORES, FREE HOSTAGES 25 MILES

FARMER UNION EVADES ISSUE, MULLIN AVERS

Bandits' Captives

Senator's Counsel Declares Rival Attorney Is Shunning Real Points.

Davis Moves to Impeach Testimony of Chamber Witness Who Fled.

Townspeople Ignore Ringing Burglar Gong, Thinking It's Fire Alarm.

Men Answering Six Robbers Description Traced to Minneapolis.

Mart Dunning, watchman at a garage, and Night Marshal Frank Whitney, inset, were overpowered and abducted by the bandits who

casts of the raid were sent out to all police officers in the state."
When all was said and done the daring raid had resulted in a couple hundred dollars in cash, and a few thousand dollars in merchandise. Perhaps realizing that they had escaped death, Dunning and Whitney told the newspapers that neither of them could give a complete description of the six armed bandits. The witnesses did recall that all of the men were well dressed, and that four of the bandits were wearing caps, while the other two were sporting light hats. The *Minneapolis Journal* wrote, "The bandits were careful to keep their captives' backs towards them. They were armed with four sawedoff shotguns and each carried a pistol." The case remained unsolved, and it wasn't until years later that it was discovered that the Barker-Karpis gang was responsible for the crimes.

On my adventure to Cambridge I started to retrace the exact steps that the Barker-Karpis had taken so many years ago. My first stop was at the Gillespie Garage, which remarkably is still a functioning auto garage. The staff was more than happy to show me around the place, pointing out where the robbers would have entered, and how the cars were most likely lined up. After visiting the buildings where the crimes took place I inevitably ended up at the Historical Society. There I had the pleasure of talking with Paul Whitney, the grandson of Marshal Whitney. I was really excited to talk with Paul because with each passing year it gets more difficult to find those who personally knew the people involved in these cases. Their personal remembrances bring the story to life in a manner that no printed page can ever compete with. Paul was quite familiar with his grandfather's history. Paul remembered that his grandfather only occasionally spoke of his frightening ordeal. When he did speak of the event, he always expressed how grateful he was just to have survived the ordeal. Paul confirmed that his grandfather was indeed armed on that fateful evening, but was taken by surprise by the gang because he never expected such a daring crime to unfold in Cambridge.

Tommy Gun Adventures:

You can still follow in the footsteps of the Barker-Karpis gang. First pull your car into the alleyway of Doctor Monte's Auto. Park your car there and walk down Main Street toward the Tack

Store. From there follow along toward the sports store, these are the buildings that were robbed. Although the businesses have changed from 1932, the buildings remain much the same allowing you the opportunity to get a feel of what the town was like back then. Once you have gathered up your merchandise (hopefully legally purchased) make your way back to Doctor Monte's Auto. Hop back in your car and head south on Highway 65, and as you approach Coopers Corner be sure to keep an eye out for any released hostages.

.

Class Play

Penrod, son Diehl, and Oliver Johnson guests at the home of s. H. E. Hoffman, Minnetonka.

g they thoroughly or high school play, s of Hawaii," staged of the Waysatta heir auditorium. It good. Harold Linde ading roles and took ly well. He is the art Linde and lives Mrs. Hoffman. Mr. unday guest at the

Dakota County Deputy Races Dillinger Gang Car 20 Miles; Bandit Wounded In Gun Fight

Deputy Sheriff Joe Heinen of Rosemount has ridden with death at his shoulder more than once but not often has he pursued so dangerous a trio of outlaws as the three Dillinger gang gunmen with whom he and three companion officers staged a running gun battle between Langdon and St. Paul Park Monday morning.

Roaring up the pavement in pursuit the gangsters' deputies men, with Deputies Dunn, the Dakota and Mr. Mee, a Hastings policeman, endeavored to halt the speeding car ahead with a few warning bullets as the cars neared Langdon. nom after the muzzle of a gun ... how ... bullets whistled around the officers' car. Only by a rare bit of luck did the pursuing party escape unscathed for one of the bullets from the gangsters' gun ripped into the visor above the windshield of Heinen's car and buried itself in the framework of the vehicle. Had the missile struck four inches lower, it would undoubtedly have penetrated the windshield behind which the alert Dakota county deputy was gripping the steering wheel of his sedan as the car raced up the pavement at a 70-mile an hour clip, on the heels of the fleeing gangsters.

Luckily the "breaks" were with the officers of the law, however, for it was one of the gangsters who stopped the only bullet that found a human target during the running gun

"JOE" HEINEN

battle. And it was Officer McArdle's 30-30 rifle that sent the bullet crashing into the rear of the fleeing coupe and, presumably, inflicted a mortal wound to one of the three gangsters in the vehicle.

Deputy Sheriff Heinen was so busily engaged with the task of keeping his car on the pavement, at the terrific speed they were traveling, that he had no opportunity to fire at their quarry. He did do some excellent work at the steering wheel, however, and would undoubtedly have overtaken the gangsters near Newport had they not swung off the pavement at St. Paul Park, and later evaded the pursuing posse in the winding hills northwest of Cottage Grove.

Kittenball Will Open le May 7th

r a six-team city were drawn up last g at a meeting of the various organi comprise the league. re enrolled in the ay were the Com y's, Crescents, Hud ardian Angels and rews. The opening kittenball campaign nday, May 7, with and Mullany troops rural fracas. Mon and Thursday eve for the tri-weekly ments and it was plit season," sched pted, with the win half meeting the ond half in a play itle. eries will end June half will start June r a two weeks' ib n halves for the earrange their line and get ready for x .weeks' struggle championship and a r pennant ings, it was decid y night meeting of thusiasts, that: shall be known as ll League. eason" will be di lves of five games of the first half to

LEGION AUXILIARY HAS APRIL MEETING

A regular meeting of Nelson-Lucking Unit, American Legion Auxiliary was held Monday afternoon, April 23 at the home of Mrs. Anna Graus, Mrs. C. L. Graus assisting.

A splendid report of the Spring Conference in Minneapolis was given by Mrs. C. R. Olson; a report on recent legislation was given by Mrs. A. B. Heinen, legislative chair-

Poppy Day and a 15 cent lunch will be served at the Community club rooms.

The May 21st meeting will be held at the home of Mrs. J. E. Oye, with Mrs. George Bye assisting.

AUCTION SALE!

Hastings Road Block Shootout – Hamilton's Last Ride

Location:

Highway 61

Hastings, MN 55033

Directions:

From Hastings, head north on Highway 61 over the bridge that spans the Mississippi River. This is where the gun battle started. As you head north toward St. Paul you will be following in the tracks of the Dillinger gang.

Gangster Lore:

Although having been caught by police several times throughout his life, John Dillinger displayed an uncanny ability to allude and escape the authorities' best laid traps. All too frequently the police were on the verge of apprehending Dillinger when fate seemed to step in and once again spare him from capture. Some in the media called it blind luck, the general public believed he was just too clever for the police, while many others simply attributed it to divine intervention. Regardless of the cause for Dillinger's good fortune, time and bullets would both soon catch up to his gang. Although Dillinger's calm demeanor and careful planning made him nearly untouchable, the same could not be said for his colleague John "Red" Hamilton. Having been wounded nearly every time the gang encountered gunfire, it was in Hastings that Hamilton's ill luck would rear its ugly head one final time.

History:

1895 – The city of Hastings constructed a spiral bridge spanning the gap of the Mississippi River. The unique layout of the bridge was created to slow down horse traffic as it entered downtown Hastings while still providing enough room for the throngs of steamboats to pass under.

1934 – Hastings police officers chased John Dillinger and his gang. The ensuing gunfight would end up costing John Hamilton his life.

1951 – The aging spiral bridge could no longer absorb the strain that the bigger and heavier modern vehicles were putting on it. It was decided that a new more modern bridge was needed.

1951 – A new steel truss bridge was constructed just east of the outdated spiral bridge. The new bridge was designed by Sver-drup and Parcel. The old spiral bridge was preserved for some time before it was deemed too expensive to maintain and was dismantled.

2008 – After the I-35 bridge collapse in Minneapolis, an assess-ment of the Hastings bridge showed several glaring warning signs that the bridge needed to be replaced.

2010 – Construction on a new bridge is scheduled.

Investigation:
Having escaped from the infamous gun battle at Wisconsin's Lit-tle Bohemia Lodge, John Dillinger, Homer Van Meter, and John "Red" Hamilton were desperate to reach the safety of St. Paul. The fallout from the botched government raid on the secluded Wisconsin lodge guaranteed that every law enforcement agent in the Midwest would now be on the lookout for the gang. At 3:40 a.m. on April 23, 1934, the Hastings Sheriff's Department re-ceived word that the gang may try to pass through the area on their way to St. Paul. As a precaution Sheriff J. Dunn assigned Deputy Sheriffs Joe Heinen, Norman Dieters, Larry Dunn, and Night Policeman F.H. McArdle to watch over the high bridge. The men were positioned at the Finch Drug Store corner, in

Heinen's car, and for over six hours the men patiently watched as vehicles passed by without incident. Then, shortly after 10 a.m. their patience paid off, as officers spotted a coupe with three men in-

side. On their way back from Little Bohemia the gangsters had decided that the northern routes into St. Paul would have been too heavily guarded, so they turned south and headed through Hastings believing it to be an easy path to safety. Their car had entered the city from the south, and turned the corner to cross the high bridge when their luck changed.

The April 27, 1934 article in the *Hastings Gazette* reported that the passing coupe's license plate (No. 92652) had matched one of the numbers sent out from the Department of Justice. The officers, who had no means of radioing in this information, tore off in pursuit of the suspected gang. Unfortunately, a large cattle truck had slipped between the police and Dillinger. A few miles down the road the officers again spotted the wanted vehicle and the chase was back on. In order to insure that the officers were tracking the right car, the *Hastings Gazette* reported, "Officer McArdle cut loose with the first warning volley of rifle bullets that was intended to reveal, definitely, whether the occupants of the other car, a block and a half ahead, were gangsters or not." Dillinger quickly answered them when he shoved his gun out the back window and returned fire. For several miles the two speeding cars exchanged over 50 shots. The *Hastings Gazette* wrote that it was the officers who scored first blood when "One of the bullets from McArdle's high-powered rifle bored its way through the rear of the speeding coupe and apparently inflicted a serious if not mortal wound to one of the gangsters." Officer McArdle told the *Gazette*, "When the bullet hit the car the coupe seemed to wobble for a minute and we thought it was going into the ditch." Luckily for the gangsters, Homer Van Meter was a skilled driver and was somehow able to keep the vehicle on the road. In the commotion of the fierce battle the police had briefly lost sight of the car when Homer Van Meter skillfully swerved his car on a dirt path (Cemetery Road). The police zoomed right by without noticing that the gangsters had even exited the road.

Now having lost the police, the men needed to assess their damage. The police had been correct when assuming their bullet had found a home in one of the gangsters. During the raging gun fight, John Hamilton was the unlucky man hit by officer McArdle's high powered rifle. A bit thrown off by the event both Dillinger and Van Meter recognized that if Hamilton was to survive they needed to get him to a doctor as soon as possible. But in order to safely reach a doctor the men needed a fresh getaway car. With Hamilton bleeding heavily in the front seat, the men scoured the back roads desperate for a new car. The time was now past noon and the men struggled to locate a new car. Frustrated, Van Meter pulled over onto the side of the road to devise their next course of action. Finally at 12:45 the men spotted an approaching vehicle off in the distance. The car was being driven by Roy Francis, who during his lunch-break decided to take his wife and infant child on a car ride through the country side. As he drove toward the men Francis noticed Van Meter standing on the side of the road. When Francis stopped to see what the problem was, he quickly saw that Van Meter was armed. The gangsters "persuaded" Francis to let them borrow his car, and equipped with a new ride, the men quickly ditched their bloodied old car on a secluded side road. By this time the gangsters' hectic lifestyle was wearing heavily on all of them. As the most wanted men in the country, the gangsters were plagued with non-stop travel in search of safe lodging, and no matter where they went the men were constantly on guard watching for any suspicious activity. When finding out that Francis was a family man with a steady job, the gangsters' envy could hardly be contained. As though talking to a therapist, the men told Francis that he was extremely fortunate to have his lifestyle. It was a genuine comment from the tired gangsters who silently longed for a life they knew would never be.

The men were ripped out of their daydreams by the worsening condition of Hamilton in the backseat. It was decided that St. Paul would be "too hot" for the men so they turned their car toward Chicago. The police soon located the discarded blood soaked car. During their investigation, the police concluded that the bullet hole in the back of the car seat indicated that whoever was sitting on that side of the car would have been struck in the region of the kidneys. The *Hastings Gazette* wrote, "The amount

of blood lost by the wounded bandit is believed to be proof that his injuries were of a fatal nature." Once again the investigators predictions turned out to be right, when within just a few days John Hamilton would be dead. Looking back on this case, it appears that death might not have been a surprise for Hamilton. A few days before going to Little Bohemia, Hamilton had spent some time with his family up in Sault Saint Marie, Michigan. While in Michigan Hamilton told relatives that he felt it was only a matter of time before the authorities caught up with him, fearing that there was simply no place left for him to hide. Perhaps Hamilton's premonition in Michigan had prepared him for his impending death.

Tommy Gun Adventures:

The historic spiral bridge that the gangsters crossed is no longer in Hastings, but you can still retrace the gun battle the Dillinger gang had with the Hastings police. Approach the town of Hastings from the south and cross the current bridge over the Mississippi. This is where the chase and gunfight began. From here you can follow the gangster's path and race your way back towards St. Paul, but be sure that no police officers are following you. If you want to see what is left of the spiral bridge, start on the south side of town and take Sibley Street toward the river until it comes to an end. From there, you can walk down to the river and see the plaque, and what is left of the stone foundation of the spiral bridge.

MAHTOMEDI
MINNESOTA

The Wildwood Killings

Location:

Wildwood Park

5 Old Wildwood Road

Mahtomedi, MN 55115

Directions:

Many of the roads around Wildwood Park have changed since 1930. From downtown Mahtomedi head southwest on Wildwood Road (244) for a few blocks and turn right on Birchwood. This is the approximate area where the bodies were found. The Wildwood Amusement Park hugged White Bear Lake. (The bodies of the gangsters were discovered one-half mile southeast of the former park.)

Gangster Lore:

To put it mildly, gangsters were a very fickle bunch. In a split second these men could turn from a jovial guy buying a round of drinks at the speakeasy to a conscienceless killer mowing down innocent civilians. However, the one thing many of the gangsters prided themselves on was their loyalty to their friends. In a racket where unsavory characters flourished, being able to count on your colleagues was essential for survival. This unbreakable loyalty played out great if you happened to find yourself in a tight pinch. It was nothing for gangsters to break each other out of jail and prison, provide safe hideouts, loan each other money, and even kill for one another. However, if you made an ill-fated decision to break this trust, the consequences would often be fatal, as evidenced by this case.

History:

1899 – The Twin City Rail Transit Company established the Wildwood Amusement Park and picnic grounds to go along with their regular streetcar service. The park contained several thrilling rides, but the main attraction was the roller coaster.

1930 – On July 15, the Bank of Willmar was robbed of nearly $100,000 in cash and bonds.

1930 – On August 13, authorities found the bodies of three murdered gangsters near Wildwood Amusement Park in Mahtomedi, MN.

1932 – Like so many other amusement parks around the county, the Wildwood Park was forced to close due to a sharp decrease in attendance.

1938 – The Wildwood Amusement Park was dismantled and the land was slated for development.

Investigation:

Like many crimes of the era, the bank robbery that took place in Willmar, MN during 1930 was never officially solved. Today it is widely believed that five men (Sammy Silverman, George "Machine Gun" Kelly, Robert Steinhardt, Harvey Bailey and Verne Miller) were the ones who helped themselves to the bank's money. Within one month of securing his share of the Willmar robbery, Sammy Silverman would end up dead in a small town outside of the Twin Cities. However, Sammy did not meet his fate alone, he was joined in death by two additional dead bodies that were found with him. Authorities identified two of the bodies as being gangsters Sammy Stein (Silverman) and Frank Colman. The third body was a bit more difficult for authorities to identify. Initially the unidentified body was thought to be that of Adolph (Butch) Myers or even Sam Hessell. The *St. Paul Dispatch* noted, "identification of this victim is least complete." The police had been wrong on both of their possible identifications, as the unidentified body turned out to be that of Mike Rusick. The police quickly sought to understand what three dead gangsters were doing in a ditch in Minnesota. The *St. Paul Dispatch* described Sammy Stein, whose real name was Sammy Silverman, as "A 25-year-old Minneapolis North Side gunman and racketeer, who was sought by Kansas City authorities for complicity in the murder of a policeman there." Frank Coleman was also a 25-year-old man who was described in the papers as a Kansas City racketeer and associate of a big gambler in that city. The third victim, Mike Rusick, was believed to be another Kansas City gangster.

In order to piece together some understanding of why three Kansas City gangsters turned up dead in Minnesota, the police had to start at the beginning. On August 13, 1930, shortly before 11p.m., authorities were out prowling the area. The police had received multiple leads stating that the area was rife with gang-

sters using the town as a safe hideout. It was during the raid when they discovered the bullet-ridden bodies of Colman and Rusick approximately one-half mile south of the amusement park at Wildwood.

During the night the police passed by a small sedan on the side of the road with its engine idling and lights burning. General Rhinow told the *St. Paul Dispatch*, "We didn't pay much attention to it at first. About five hundred yards south we decided to swing back and investigate. We stopped the car and got out. On the left side of the car we found Myers (Rusick) dead. He had been shot in the back of the head. With our flashlights we discovered blood stains on the grass a short distance from where the dead man was found. After searching for a short time Coleman was found in a swale about 25 yards from the car. He had crawled down there, it was evident from the trail he had left. Coleman was unconscious, so he was loaded into a car and taken to St. John's Hospital in St. Paul." In fact, Coleman was so severely injured that he died later that evening. The next morning at 6 a.m. several Wildwood residents discovered the bloody body of a third unidentified man. The witnesses told the *St. Paul Dispatch*, "We were riding back to Wildwood from St. Paul in a truck. Coming down the hill we saw a man sitting by a tree. He looked as if he were just resting. When we got even with the tree we soon learned what had happened." What they had stumbled upon was Sammy Silverman's bloodied body. Silverman was discovered sitting upright near a willow tree about ten feet from the roadside. Newspapers stated that his left arm was draped over a low bough which functioned like a crutch that held up his body. Silverman had been shot twice. One bullet had entered his head from behind the right ear and passed through his right eye, it then bored its way through his left arm. The second bullet had been fired directly into his neck, seemingly just for good measure. Outside of the dead bodies, the authorities had little evidence to go on. Near the body of Silverman, authorities discovered a .32 caliber automatic pistol with its safety still on. Several discharged cartridges also littered the area near the bodies of the bloody men. In addition to the spent cartridges, the police found a gallon of gasoline. The discovery of the gasoline led authorities to the conclusion that the killers may have been planning to cremate their victims before someone or something frightened them away. The abandoned car, which was thought to have been stolen, had the Missouri license plate number 383-711.

News of the murders spread quickly, and the lack of any substantial evidence prompted many newspapers to speculate on the reason for the killings. The *St. Paul Pioneer Press* wrote that the notorious Chicago gangster Bugs Moran, who was thought to be in Minnesota at the time, may have been connected to the killings. Other newspapers tried to pin the murders on Al Capone, who was also thought to be visiting Minnesota during the time span of the killing. The *St. Paul Dispatch* offered up a theory that rang the truest when they suggested that perhaps some type of illegal deal had gone terribly wrong. General Rhinow told the *Dispatch*, "Stein and the others may have been mixed up in the Willmar bank robbery and killed in a disagreement over splitting the loot." Providing some insight into the murder itself, an operative on the case told the *Dispatch*, "It looks to me like a one-man job. All three of the victims were shot in the back of the head. I think one man who sat in the back of the car, did the shooting with an automatic pistol." Despite the appearance of a thorough formal investigation, the case was

never officially solved. However, Paul Maccabee wrote in his book, *John Dillinger Slept Here*, that during an interview with police, "Machine Gun" Kelly identified Verne Miller as the killer of the three men. Verne Miller and Sammy Silverman had been

part of the gang that robbed the bank in Willmar just a few
months prior. Machine Gun Kelly alleged that Silverman had
made the ill-fated decision to try and double cross Miller when it
came to the splitting of the loot. Apparently Miller did not appre-
ciate the lopsided arrangement and decided to take Silverman,
and his two friends, out for good.

Tommy Gun Adventures:
Although the area has changed significantly over the years (It is
now littered with lakeside homes) you still can travel to the
southeast corner of White Bear Lake to where the plaque of the
Wildwood Amusement Park rests. From here you can drive the
half mile toward Highway 244 and you will be in the area of the
gangster killings of 1930.

DR. MAY SAYS HE WAS FORCED BY DILLINGER

Police Hunting "Babyface" Nelson in Wisconsin Timberland and St. Paul—Evelyn Frechette Had Keys to Hollywood Jail.

St. Paul, April 27.—(AP)—The law snapped without effect today at the heels of another Dillinger gangster as George (Baby Face) Nelson, one of the most desperate, staged an escape nearly as startling as those for which his chief has become notorious.

Striking back when the law almost closed around him in the Indian shack of Ollie Catfish in the Lac du Flambeau region of northern Wisconsin, Nelson, named as the killer of a federal agent pursuing Dillinger, stole and auto and ran a gauntlet of deer rifles, shotguns and pistols near Fifield, Wis.

Authorities believed Nelson had escaped but they kept a watch at every highway, bridge and railroad throughout the territory on the possibility that he and perhaps other members of the gang had found a new hideout in the tall timber.

There was also a possibility he had reached St. Paul since police cars here broadcast a warning to all squad cars to pick up the car in which Nelson was believed traveling.

New evidence of the foolhardy daring of Dillinger and his cohorts came simultaneously with the the story of how the outlaw and his companions forced Dr. Clayton E. May. Minneapolis physician, to administer to a bullet wound in Dillinger for four days, keeping the physician under constant guard and often threatening his life.

40

Largest Robbery in Minnesota History:
Northwestern National Bank

Location:

1223 North Washington Avenue

Minneapolis, MN 55401

Directions:

Take Plymouth Ave. NE to the west toward Interstate 94. Turn left on Washington Ave. N (Highway 52) and the former location of the bank will be on your right. The bank sat approximately between the buildings that now house the Geek Squad and the Lerner Distribution Center.

Gangster Lore:

While hiding out in St. Paul under the protection of crooked cops, the Barker-Karpis Gang hatched the idea of robbing the Northwestern National Bank in Minneapolis. From the living room of their rented Robert Street home, the gang produced a meticulously thought out plan on how they would rid the bank of its money.

History:

1932 – Fred Barker, Alvin Karpis, Tommy Holden, Bernard Phillips, and Larry De Vol robbed the Northwestern National Bank.

Currently – The bank is no longer there; instead a new building houses the Geek Squad Company.

Investigation:

On March 29, 1932, the Barker-Karpis Gang pulled up near the Northwestern National Bank to make a large withdrawal. Actually, the gang was looking to withdraw every single penny the bank had. The men involved that day were Fred Barker, Alvin Karpis, Tommy Holden, Bernard Phillips and Larry De Vol. Armed with machine guns, the men must had made an imposing impression on the customers, because numerous newspapers around the U.S., including the *Van Wert Daily Bulletin*, reported that there were not five, but seven men involved in the robbery.

The March 29 issue of the *Modesto News-Herald* wrote, "Eighteen officials and employees and six customers were forced to lie on the floor, after the bandits threatened to shoot them unless J. A. Junz, manager, opened the vault." During the robbery all of the gang's initial planning efforts paid off, as later that day the *Chester Times* reported, "The robbery was so carefully planned out that the entire bank's personnel were taken by surprise and herded into a back room before the muzzles of submachine guns and sawed off shotguns."

Once the men had drained the vaults of the cash and bonds, the gang causally walked through the back door using two female employees as shields. The police originally believed that the gang had incorporated a decoy car into their plans, as the *United Press* wrote, "This car drove through a traffic sign and as the policeman attempted to halt this car, the second with the robbers drove up to the bank." A few days later, reports began to surface

that the first traffic violation was simply a fortunate coincidence that allowed the robbers to enter the bank undetected.

Just how much money the gang had gotten away with varied from source to source. The *Florence Morning News* quoted the bank's president E. W. Decker as saying "The exact amount of securities taken, nearly all of which were bonds, could not be determined until a thorough examination of records was made." The *San Antonio Express* claimed that the bank had lost over "$50,000 in cash, and approximately $150,000 in securities." Once out of the bank, the gang retreated back to the safety of St. Paul, and used their Robert Street rental to count out and divide their loot. The whole bank robbery had lasted less than 10 minutes. The gangsters had gotten away without firing one single gun shot, however, one bank customer did claim that he was slugged by one of the robbers. The only real piece of evidence left for investigators was a hat that the *Salt Lake Tribune* said was "dropped in the flight," and that it bore "a haberdasher's inscription, 'Al Baskin, Joliet Ill.'" However, on April 3, the *Syracuse Herald* ran a story titled "Former Policeman Revealed as Bandit." The article tells that Bernard Phillips, a former motorcycle policeman, had been identified as one of the gunmen. Witnesses also identified Clyde Bridges, who was not there, as another of the robbers.

Tommy Gun Adventures:
The large parking lot where the former bank operated makes a perfect tour destination, as you can walk around the area and imagine life as it was in 1932.

Dr. May's Underground Clinic

Location:

1835 Park Avenue

Minneapolis, MN 55404

Private property – view from road

Directions:

The former clinic is located on the intersection of Park Ave. and
E 19th St. From E. Franklin Ave. turn North on Park Ave. and the
rental building will be on your right.

Gangster Lore:

During the 1920s and 30s if you wanted certain medical treat-
ments or procedures that were either illegal or socially sensitive

you had to seek out the services of a doctor that would be willing to treat you in a private setting. For the right price these doctors would treat all sorts of venereal diseases, perform illegal abortions, and even patch up the aftermath of a fight, stabbing, or shooting. You can imagine that these doctors were kept quite busy by the frequent business from the city's numerous underworld characters. However, treating men wanted by the authorities did not come without its risks, as Dr. May would soon discover.

History:
1908 – The building on Park Avenue was constructed.

1930s – Dr. Clayton May ran an underground clinic out of the building. The clinic also provided an apartment where his nurse Augusta Salt lived.

1934 – John Dillinger stayed at the clinic while recovering from a gun fight with the authorities.

Currently – The building is currently being used for condominiums.

Investigation:
During the raid and subsequent shootout at the Lincoln Court Apartments, John Dillinger was struck in the leg by a passing bullet. The bullet had torn right through his leg, and although the wound was not life-threatening it was severe enough to force

Dillinger to seek medical attention. However, since Dillinger was one of the most famous fugitives in the world, he could not simply stroll into the local hospital seeking help. He needed someone who could be trusted, someone who would not turn him in. Luckily for Dillinger, his friend Eddie Green knew of a doctor who operated with extreme discretion when treating special patients. Based on firsthand experience, Green knew that it would be safe to send Dillinger to Dr. May. Dr. Clayton May was an established doctor who had been practicing medicine for many years throughout Minneapolis. Even more fortuitous was the fact that in addition to his conventional practice, Dr. May also ran a private "clinic" out of a small apartment in Minneapolis where he performed abortions, treated venereal diseases, and conducted a variety of other procedures that brought him a nice little profit. Seeing that Dillinger needed quick medical treatment, Green immediately contacted Dr. May who agreed to look at Green's "special patient." On March 31, Dillinger limped into Dr. May's back office with his arm around girlfriend Billie Frechette. Dillinger was vaguely claiming that he had been injured in an explosion. Dr. May took a look at the bloodied leg and first thought that it was some type of knife wound, but as he cut away Dillinger's bloody pants, he saw that a bullet had entered and exited the leg. Not one to ask unnecessary questions, Dr. May quickly cleaned and bandaged up the wound and informed his patient that he was welcome to stay and recover for a long as he needed. Later that evening, perhaps recognizing that his special patient was John Dillinger, Dr. May sought out Eddie Green and re-negotiated the much higher service fee of $500.

Dillinger and Billie holed up in the apartment while the nurse, Augusta Salt, tended to Dillinger's leg wound. Finally after several days Dillinger's leg had healed up enough to make travel possible. Dillinger and Billie were anxious to get out of the Twin Cities and on April 4, under the cover of darkness, they set off for Indiana to attend a Dillinger family reunion. In all of their excitement they had somehow "forgotten" to pay their bill.

While Dillinger and Billie headed off to see family, Dr. May did not get away so easily. The authorities soon discovered that Dillinger had been treated at Dr. May's Park Ave. clinic. In what was a new found effort by the FBI to flush out the gangsters by cracking down hard on those who aided them, both Dr. May and Nurse Salt were arrested on the charges of conspiracy to harbor and conceal John Dillinger. After his arrest, newspapers around the country ran an interview with Dr. May conducted by reporter Jack Mackay. From the inside of his Ramsey County jail cell Dr. May held strong to his assertion that he had been forced at gunpoint to treat the injured man. Whether completely true or not, Dr. May felt playing the helpless doctor held hostage card was his only option. The *Albert Lea Evening Tribune* reported that as soon as Dr. May met the injured man he was staring down the barrel of a Tommy Gun. Dr. May told the newspa-

Sent To Prison

Dr. Clayton E. May, above, who treated John Dillinger for a leg wound, was found guilty today, along with Evelyn Frechette, of a conspiracy to harbor the notorious bandit. Dr. May was sentenced for two years and fined $1,000.

per, "He warned me that my life 'wouldn't be worth a cent' if I did not follow orders. He had a cynical smile on his face, and I could tell by the look in his eye that he meant business and feared he would carry out his threats if I refused." Although Dr. May was trembling with fear while recalling the events, the jury did not find his version of events very credible, and soon pronounced him guilty as charged. Judge Gunnar Nordbye sentenced Dr. May to two years imprisonment and issued him a $1,000 fine. His co-defendant Nurse Salt, had a bit more luck, or sympathy, and was found not guilty and was released.

The Bloody Robbery of the
Third Northwestern National Bank

Location:

430 East Hennepin Avenue

Minneapolis, MN 55414

Directions:

From downtown, take Hennepin Avenue toward University Avenue. At the intersection of Hennepin and Central you will see the triangle shaped parking lot with the Galapagos Market (420 E Hennepin) in it. The bank originally sat where the parking lot is now located.

Gangster Lore:

As far as daring 1930s bank robberies go, the Third Northwestern National Bank robbery ranks right up there with the best of them. First of all, the bank was positioned on the extremely busy corner of Central Avenue and Hennepin Avenue. This popular location created several possible problems for the gangsters. Beside the fact that hundreds of witnesses would be mulling around in the area, the heavy vehicle and street car traffic would most certainly hamper any plans for a fast getaway. Adding to the mounting danger was the fact that the bank was constructed with a lot of glass that allowed the outside world to see nearly everything that was transpiring inside.

So with a myriad of security concerns why did the gang decided to rob this bank? Well, with years of criminal experience behind them, maybe the gang enjoyed a supreme confidence that their skills couldn't be matched. Or perhaps the grind of their career, even if it was robbing banks, had grown tedious and the men were seeking some new challenge and excitement to rejuvenate them. Regardless of their motives, the gang disregarded the obvious obstacles and decided that the benefits of robbing the bank would far outweigh the risk. As fate would have it, the robbers could not have been more wrong.

History:

1932 – The Barker gang robbed the Third Northwestern Bank. On December 17, the *Appleton Post-Crescent* wrote that "Detective Captain Frank Forestal expressed the opinion the raiders were members of a Kansas City 'mob' which police assert robbed another bank of the Northwestern group here in March. Forestal said his men were hunting Mike Aliegretto, 32; Sam Hunt, 31; James Hines, 26; Ralph Pierce, 25; and Clyde Bridges, 28, all of Kansas City." None of the men the police were hunting were involved in the bank robbery. It is not known if this faulty information was given intentionally as part of the protection given to the Barker gang under the O'Connor System, or if was just simply the early stages of the police work.

Investigation:
On December 16, Fred and Doc Barker, accompanied by Jess Doyle, Verne Miller, William Weaver, Larry De Vol, and Alvin Karpis, approached the busy bank intent on robbing it. The bank had two entrances and as two men entered through the Central Avenue door, two others went through the Hennepin Avenue entrance. The fifth man armed with a machine gun, remained outside as the watchman (De Vol). At the time of the robbery the bank was filled with ten employees and six patrons. Having watched the bank for many days, the gangsters knew the inner workings of the staff pretty well. This information was put to use when a teller tried to lie to the gang, stating that he was unable to open up the vault. The man was quickly pistol whipped in the head for his deception. Amazingly, during the midst of all the commotion and excitement, two employees had the wherewithal to trigger the silent alarm that was wired to the police station. The first officers to respond to the alarm were Ira Evans and Leo Gorski. The two men pulled up just as three of the robbers were

exiting the bank with bags of money. Unfortunately the officers stood no chance in apprehending the robbers, all of whom were stone-cold killers. The *Albert Lea Evening Tribune* stated, "Evans and Gorski were mowed down by a withering blast of machine gun fire as they drove up to the bank in a police radio car." Patrolman Evans took the worst of the barrage and the spray of machine gun bullets killed him instantly. Officer Gorski was riddled with at least five bullets, and the *Modesto News-Herald* claimed that he "had only a slight chance of recovery." Sadly the medical predictions were accurate, and two days later Officer Gorski died from his bullet wounds.

During the robbery the gang had scooped up over $20,000 in cash and nearly $100,000 in securities and stuffed it all into their getaway car. However, sometime during the all of the frantic shooting, a stray bullet had blown out a tire on their getaway car. With three good tires, the gang sped off toward a second getaway car they had previously stashed in Como Park. With their adrenaline still pumping from their shootout, the robbers stopped to transfer their bank haul into their fresh car. What had already been a bloody day was about to get even bloodier.

Tommy Gun Adventures:

The area where Third Northwestern National Bank stood is now a parking lot for the Galapagos Market. As you stand in the parking lot you can envision the danger that the two busy streets posed for the robbers. Local legend also states that bullet holes from the gunfight can still be observed at Arone's Bar across the street.

REDWOOD FALLS
MINNESOTA

Citizens State Bank Robbery

Location:

140 E. 2nd Street

Redwood Falls, MN 56283

Directions:

The old bank building sits in Redwood Falls' quaint downtown. The bank building is on 2nd Street, and is currently occupied by Johnson Surplus.

Gangster Lore:

In 1932, Redwood Falls was a quiet rural farming community located nearly three hours west of the Twin Cities. The small town enjoyed flourishing downtown businesses, and was able to support three profitable banks. One of these banks, the Citizens State Bank, took great pride in the fact that it had been capitalized at $100,000. Customers took comfort in the fact that the bank was one of the largest small town banks in the entire state. During this time many rural families were still a bit untrusting of banks, and this kind of strength and stability helped attract, and calm, many weary customers. Of course, the bank's success also attracted the attention of the Barker-Karpis gang, whose "business" the bank would rather do without.

History:
1932 – The Barker-Karpis gang stole nearly $35,000 from the Citizen State Bank.

2001 – The Redwood Gazette, the newspaper that had occupied the building for many years, moved to a new location leaving the building empty.

2001-2008 – During this time the building sat vacant, looking for a new tenant.

2008 – Johnson Surplus store moved into the building selling clothing, furniture, and skateboarding gear.

Currently – The building is occupied by the Johnson Surplus store. Several unique fixtures from the bank are still located inside the store.

Investigation:

On September 23, 1932, the Barker-Karpis gang pulled into the rural town of Redwood Falls intent on leaving with more money than they had arrived with. To help fulfill their intentions, the men were preparing to "politely" ask the bank for its money. Perhaps to fit in among the rural farmers, the men were all clad in brand new overalls. Well, not exactly, as the *Ames Daily Tribune-Times* wrote that the men were "Disguised in blue denim overalls over their expensive clothes." With their weird semi-disguises in place, the men entered the bank at 9:15a.m and presented the teller with a bill that they wished to have changed. At that moment the three other men, who had been waiting in the hallway, slowly moved into the bank. According to the *Oelwein Daily Register* one of the men announced, "This is a holdup! Keep Quiet." To help speed up their request, the gangsters brandished shiny automatic pistols. To avoid being detected by any pedestrians, the bank employees were quickly told to lie down on the floor. The *Oelwein Daily Register* reported that several of the

staff, perhaps not realizing the deadly capabilities of the robbers, hesitated, forcing one of the gang members to give E.W. Whiting these words of encouragement: "Get down now! Don't peek or you'll lose your head." Once the nearly $35,000 was packed into the sacks, the gang headed for the back door of the building to their waiting large Buick sedan. In order to prevent any brave police officers from firing at them, several employees were chosen to serve as human shields. The *Rhinelander Daily News* reported, that "They hurried out through a rear door taking Art Hassenstab, cashier, and Miss Mona Leavens, his secretary with them." The two hostages were guaranteed that if they did exactly as they were told, they would not be harmed.

To help protect the men Miss Leavens was forced to stand on the car's running board right next to the driver. In an embellished recap of the event, the *Rhinelander Daily News* quoted Miss Leavens saying "the driver held onto me with his left hand and drove with the other. He used profane language several times and told me to do be sure and look the other way if I didn't want my hand to get broken." Once the gang had made a clear getaway, the unharmed hostages were thrown out of the car approximately two miles outside of town. Stranded on the road, Mr. Hassenstab flagged down a passing motorist, who gave the two hostages a ride back into town, where they alerted the police to the gang's route.

Even with their exhaustive planning, the gang could not prevent witnesses from viewing their work. Adjoining the bank building

was the Fox Millinery, whose owner Mrs. Cora Fox, and her employee, Miss Matilda Buchholtz, were treated with front row
seats to the action. The *Redwood Gazette* reported that the
women "First noticed strange men carrying sacks to a car parked
behind the bank. Miss Buchholtz remarked that 'if we had a gun
we could shoot them.' Just at that moment one of the bandits,
who was acting as a sentry, stuck his head out of the door and
calmly remarked 'you wouldn't shoot us would you?'" As soon
as the gangsters were safely out of sight the alarm was raised.
The *Redwood County Sun* reported, "Within five minutes of the
robbery a notice was sent out over several radio stations in this
part of the country to be on the lookout for the bandits." A few
minutes after the radio announcements were broadcast, Sheriff
L.J. Kise, and his son, Douglas, headed south in pursuit of the
robbers. Sheriff Kise also immediately ordered his airplane into
the sky to help aid in the pursuit. After traveling just a couple of
miles in his car, the sheriff's efforts were quickly thwarted by
three large roofing nails found in their tires. It was common
practice for bank robbers to carry buckets of small roofing nails
which they would scatter across the road, thus ensuring that any
pursing vehicle would be sidelined with punctured tires.

During my research into this robbery I was fortunate enough to
meet up with Redwood Falls' Mayor, Gary Revier. Gary had
done some extensive research into the crime, and provided me
with a wealth of information on the robbery. In Gary's possession was the original 1932 typed letter from bank hostage Miss
Leavens, in which she accurately recorded the details of the rob-

bery. Contrary to all of the sensational media accounts of the robbery, Miss Leavens stated that right after the robbery occurred
she received a call from a Twin Cities reporter. Still a bit shaken
from the ordeal, and not sure what the bank's protocol was, she
politely declined the interviewer's request. A bit naïve on the
shady practices of some newspaper men, she was surprised to
read statements attributed to her in the papers. Miss Leavens
wrote, "When the paper came out it was quite an interview and
not much truth in it." Miss Leavens also wrote in her letter that
the only time she heard the men use profanity was when they
were dropping the two hostages off. Apparently the gangsters
thought Mr. Hassenstab was taking too much time jumping off
from the running board, for which the gangsters told him, "Get
off you son-of-a-bitch."

Like so many similar cases of the time, the exact identities of the
robbers were never known. Most likely the group of bandits was

made up of Fred Barker, Alvin Karpis, Tommy Holden, Bernard Phillips, and Larry De Vol. It appears that Alvin Karpis was again the mastermind behind the detailed planning of the robbery. The *Brainerd Daily Dispatch* wrote, "The bandits apparently had studied a plat of the bank before the holdup and knew where every bit of money in the bank was kept." The crime would go down as one of the gang's smoothest, as the whole robbery lasted less than five minutes, and not a single gun shot was fired.

Tommy Gun Adventures:
You can follow in the footsteps of the Barker-Karpis gang and retrace their robbery. The bank building is still recognizable from the street. Although Johnson Surplus is the current tenant, a lot of the bank's old structures are still inside the building. When you stop in you can still see the original night deposit slot and safe, and if you walk back to where the original bank vault was, you can still see the vault's solid concrete wall and breathing pipes.

You can also park your car in the alley behind the old bank building and walk out the back door and follow the escape route of the Barker-Karpis gang. Head west for half a block until you reach S. Mill Street, turn right (the gangsters turned left, but it is now a one-way street), and make a U-turn and head south to 3rd Street where you will turn west (right). Drive to Minnesota Street and turn south (left) to Flynn Street. From Flynn you can hop on to old Highway 71 and make your getaway to your safe hideout in St. Paul.

ROCHESTER
MINNESOTA

The Release of Edward Bremer

Location:

Highway 63 (South Broadway)

Rochester, MN

Directions:

The exact location where Edward Bremer was released is not known. Bremer believed that he was released shortly after passing over a bridge, and that he also passed a wooded lot. This information lead Rochester newspapers to speculate that he was released on South Broadway (Highway 63). However, other Rochester residents pointed out that both Highway 50 and 55 pass over bridges near the city as well.

Your best bet in retracing the Bremer release is to travel into Rochester from the south on Highway 63 and head through town, knowing that Bremer most likely made the same route. You can also continue along Bremer's route by driving to Owatonna and then set off for St. Paul.

Gangster Lore:
The gangsters that participated in kidnappings prided themselves on the magnificent effort exerted in the planning of the actual crimes. Months of detailed work would hopefully pay off through a successful kidnapping. No detail, no matter how minor, was left unchecked. Inside the mind of the gangsters, the possibility of being caught was nearly unthinkable. Yet, when the Barker-Karpis gang kidnapped Edward Bremer, they made several crucial mistakes that would lead to their downfall…the first being that they chose Edward Bremer.

History:
1933 – The Barker-Karpis gang successfully kidnapped William Hamm and was paid the $100,000 ransom before releasing him unharmed.

1934 – The Barker-Karpis gang kidnapped bank president Edward Bremer while he was on his morning drive to work. Bremer was the son of Adolph Bremer, who headed the Jacob Schmidt Brewery Company. Bremer was also the nephew of Otto Bremer, who was a prominent banker and business man with political connections that reached the White House.

1934 – On February 7, the Barker-Karpis gang released Edward Bremer in Rochester Minnesota.

Investigation:

On February 7, 1934, after the Barker-Karpis gang had secured the $200,000 ransom payment in Zumbrota Minnesota, they released Edward Bremer. Their prisoner had been held hostage in Illinois since his kidnapping in St. Paul on January 17. Just exactly where Bremer was released is not known, the February 8th edition of the *Rochester Post-Bulletin* reported that Police Chief Louis Claude and a Justice Department operative had investigated several roads into the city, but failed to find any trace of the scene of Bremer's release. The paper stated, "Police were reported to have sought goggles and eye bandages worn by Bremer, who was understood to have said he threw them away." What is known about Bremer's release is that a little before 8 p.m. on the night of the 7th, Bremer was pushed out of the gang's car into the middle of the street near downtown Rochester. The FBI report on the Barker gang stated, "Mr. Bremer was in-

structed by them to get out of the car in the middle of the street and to stand with his back towards the direction in which the kidnappers' car was headed. He was then told to count slowly to fifteen, after which the bandage over his eyes could be removed."

During his release Bremer was given verbal directions to the bus station and at 8:07 p.m. Bremer arrived at the Rochester bus station. By this time, the news of the high profile kidnap-

ping had been on the minds of everyone, yet as the disoriented Bremer wandered the streets and bus stations he was not recognized by anyone. With all things being considered, Bremer was in fairly good physical condition when he approached the ticket booth. When the teller informed him that he had just missed the last bus for the Twin Cities, Bremer became highly agitated. The cashier that had assisted him, Mrs. Jennie Haight, later told the Rochester Post-Bulletin, "The man was well dressed in good clothes." She also stated that Bremer had a small mustache and she remarked on the "peculiar condition of his eyes," which had been blindfolded by bandages for nearly three weeks. Perhaps sensing Bremer's desperation, Mrs. Haight quickly called a cab to transport Bremer to the Chicago and Northwestern train station, where arrangements had been made to delay departure of the train to Owatonna to accommodate the late passenger. Once inside the train station, Bremer was sold his ticket by another cashier, L.J. Moser, who told the *Rochester Post-Bulletin* that he had no idea the man purchasing the ticket was Bremer. Moser stated that the man "was highly nervous and fidgeted constantly," during his brief stop at the depot. From Owatonna, Bremer caught the 9:55 bus to St. Paul and arrived home to his surprised and ecstatic family. Up until this time, the authorities, at the request of the family, had played a passive role in the release of Bremer. The family believed that any intense police involvement would trigger violent actions from the kidnappers. However, once the unharmed Bremer reached the safety of his home, the authorities were free to thoroughly pursue the kidnappers.

DIVISION OF INVESTIGATION
U. S. DEPARTMENT OF JUSTICE
WASHINGTON, D. C.

WANTED

St. Louis Park
Minnesota

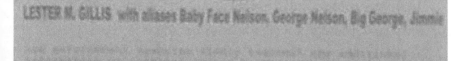

LESTER M. GILLIS with aliases Baby Face Nelson, George Nelson, Big George, Jimmie

Baby Face Nelson Goes a Killing

Location:

6001 Excelsior Blvd.

St. Louis Park, MN 55416

Directions:

The former Brookside Inn is now occupied by the Sew What business. It is located on the corner of Excelsior Blvd. and Brookside Avenue.

Gangster Lore:

Baby Face Nelson is truly a character study in duality. On one hand, Nelson was often described as being polite, well-mannered, friendly, conversational, and jovial. Even as a child strangers picked up on his good manners. Throughout his time in juvenile detention centers his caretakers often noted that he could be very charming when he chose to be. His outgoing personality came through to make Nelson quite possibly the best connected gangster of his time. Nelson routinely introduced fellow criminals to one another, and in times of trouble when the "heat" was on, Nelson could be counted on to arrange a safe house for the men to "cool off." When no one could get their hands on fresh weapons and ammunition, Nelson regularly came through with the goods. And while nearly all of the gangsters enjoyed dating multiple women at the same time, Nelson was said to be an extremely devoted husband to his wife Helen and their two children.

Yet, do not get the wrong impression about Baby Face, because behind the polite façade, Nelson was a cold-blooded killer who would mow down anyone who dared to step in his way. Nelson earned a notorious reputation for his quick triggered temper that often ended with gunshots. Even his fellow gangsters expressed concern about his crazed antics, and many refused to work with him due to the fear of not knowing what his sporadic behavior would produce. Many bank robbery witnesses recalled seeing Nelson laughing like a maniac as he sprayed bullets into the surrounding buildings and cars. With Baby Face it was a toss-up, as you could never predict which version of him you would encounter. Unfortunately for Theodore Kidder, he ran into the negative side of Baby Face Nelson, and it cost him his life.

History:

1908 – George "Baby Face" Nelson was born Lester J. Gillis in Chicago to a middle-class family.

1921 – Growing up, Nelson always seemed to get into trouble; at the age of 13 Nelson was arrested for theft and joyriding.

1931 – Nelson was again arrested, and was sentenced to one year to life in the state prison, but Nelson knew that prison life did not suit him.

1932 – While being transported to prison Nelson attacked his guard and escaped. He would never spend another day behind bars.

1934 – While traveling in the Twin Cities, Nelson and his gang shot and killed Theodore Kidder.

1934 – On November 27, while driving through the town of Barrington, IL with his wife, Helen Gillis, and fellow crook John Paul Chase, Nelson noticed a car being driven by FBI agents passing by in the opposite direction. At the very same moment the passing agents noticed Nelson's car speeding by. Nelson, a skilled driver, immediately spun his car into a U-turn and ended up in pursuit of the FBI car. A fierce gun battle ensued, causing the FBI to swerve their car into a field to avoid oncoming traffic. Nelson's car had also suffered from the gunfight as he found himself being pursued by another set of agents. Nelson, realizing that his vehicle had little left, swung his car into the North Side Park, where it screeched to a stop. The pursuing FBI car containing agents Herman Hollis and Samuel Cowley passed by Nelson before stopping about 100 feet away. Using their car as protection, the FBI agents began blasting away at Nelson's car. Helen, scared for her life, darted off for the field while Nelson, who had already been hit, started marching directly towards the agents with his gun blazing. It was a bloody exchange where both Baby Face and the agents took heavy damage. Soon it became clear to Nelson that the agents were severely wounded, so with blood flowing from his multiple wounds, Nelson staggered his way back to the car and took off with Chase and his wife. The trio raced off in search of medical attention for Baby Face, who was riddled with bullets. Both of the FBI agents died from their wounds, and within a couple of hours, the country's most wanted man would also be dead.

Investigation:

On Sunday evening March 4, 1934, Theodore Kidding was driving home from Minneapolis accompanied by his wife and mother-in-law. As fate would have it, at the same time Kidder was driving home, Baby Face and several other gangsters were out driving in their large sedan. The official story is that while cruising along the gangsters cut directly in front of Kidder's vehicle. Angered by the gang's aggressive actions Kidder made the foolish decision to accelerate and cut right back in front of the gangsters. Mrs. Effie Duxbury, Kidder's mother-in-law, told police that she and the Kidders had just attended a birthday party at the home of a friend. It was around 10:30 p.m. when the Kidders left the Comfort's residence and headed down Lake Street. Mrs. Duxbury told the newspapers that somewhere between Lyndale Ave. and Hennepin Ave., she first noticed that a large sedan was following them. The *La Crosse Tribune* and Leader-Press wrote, "Mrs. Duxbury said the machine swept up to them, attempted to force Kidder into the curb and then followed them when Kidder succeeded outmaneuvering the car and proceeded westward to Excelsior Boulevard." Thinking that the rude incident was over, the Kidders continued on toward their home, oblivious to the threat that their actions triggered. It wasn't until they turned off the main boulevard that they noticed the aggressive car was still following them. Wisely, Kidder did not want to lead the unknown occupants of the car back to his house, so he decided to drive around the block in an effort to lose them. Kidder turned east on Lowell Ave. and drove toward a nearby restaurant called the Brookside Inn. Underestimating the ruthlessness of his pursuers, Kidder believed that the Inn's public location would provide some safety. Once Kidder stopped at the Inn, the mysterious sedan pulled up right alongside his car. Taken back by the brashness Kidder got out and walked behind his vehicle, either to go inside for help, or to confront the other car. At that very same moment a man emerged from the other car walked up to a halted Kidder, where the two engaged in a conversation. Both Kidder's wife and his mother-in-law could hear the men talking, but their voices were too low and muffled for the women to make out what was being said. The men talked for approximately thirty seconds when Mrs. Duxbury saw a weapon thrust out of the window of the other car. The silence of the night was broken with three gun blasts originating from the other car. Of the three shots, the *Brainerd Daily Dispatch* reported, "Two stuck Kidder in the abdomen." The *La Crosse Tribune* and Leader-Press wrote that after the shots "Mrs. Duxbury screamed 'What have you done?' 'Keep your damned mouth shut or we'll give it to you too,' shouted one of the men." Mrs. Kidder quickly ran inside the restaurant to get help. The gunshots had also alerted several patrons, who came out of the restaurant in time to see a man jump into the back seat of the Hudson as it sped away westward. The witnesses reported that the car had California plates. Several customers rushed over to help carry Kidder back into the restaurant. Their efforts provide futile, and within min-utes Kidder was dead.

It appeared that Kidder, a 35-year-old salesman, was just another innocent victim of the ever-increasing gangster violence. The killing should have been an open and shut case.   Yet several newspapers, including the *La Crosse Tribune* and Leader-Press, reported that a night prior to his death, a car with three unknown men had pulled up to Kidder's home in St. Louis Park. The paper reported, "County Attorney Edward Goff, investigating the affair, learned from neighbors about a mysterious car containing three men, was seen around the Kidder home the night before the young salesman's murder." That mysterious car had been spotted shining a light into the home, as though looking for someone. Authorities began looking into the background of Kidder, who was a salesman for the National Lead Company and had just recently moved to the St. Louis Park area. Steven Nickels and William Helmer wrote in their book, *Baby Face Nelson*, that several interesting theories were developed to explain the murder of Kidder, including the idea that he "had developed some unsavory associations in the Twin Cities." Yet Nickels and Helmer also wrote, "There is absolutely nothing linking any of the bank robbers to Kidder prior to the night of his death." However, it was discovered that Kidder also had a part time job working at Kennedy Brothers Arms Company. With his job dealing with arms it was alleged that Kidder may have helped the gangsters obtain ammunition.

Was this simply a case of deadly road rage, or was it a gang deal gone wrong? Unfortunately, the authorities had few clues to go on. The only evidence they could gather was matching the description of the Hudson sedan used by the gangsters to one that Baby Face had purchased in San Francisco a few weeks prior to the murder. Baby Face Nelson loved cars from an early age, and considered himself an expert driver, so it figures that if the mysterious car was indeed Baby Face's, he was most likely the one driving it. The list of his possible accomplices includes Homer Van Meter, John Paul Chase, Tommy Carroll, Pat Reilly, or a plethora of other underworld characters that associated with Nelson. With so little evidence to go on, this case was never solved, and the murder remains a mystery to this very day.

Tommy Gun Adventures:

Travel down Lake Street, and somewhere between Lyndale and Hennepin, be on the lookout for any mysterious vehicles following you. Head west on Excelsior Boulevard until you get to 6001, this is where the Brookside Inn was located (now Sew What). If you head to the parking lot you will be in the approximate area where Kidder was shot to death.

St. Paul Minnesota

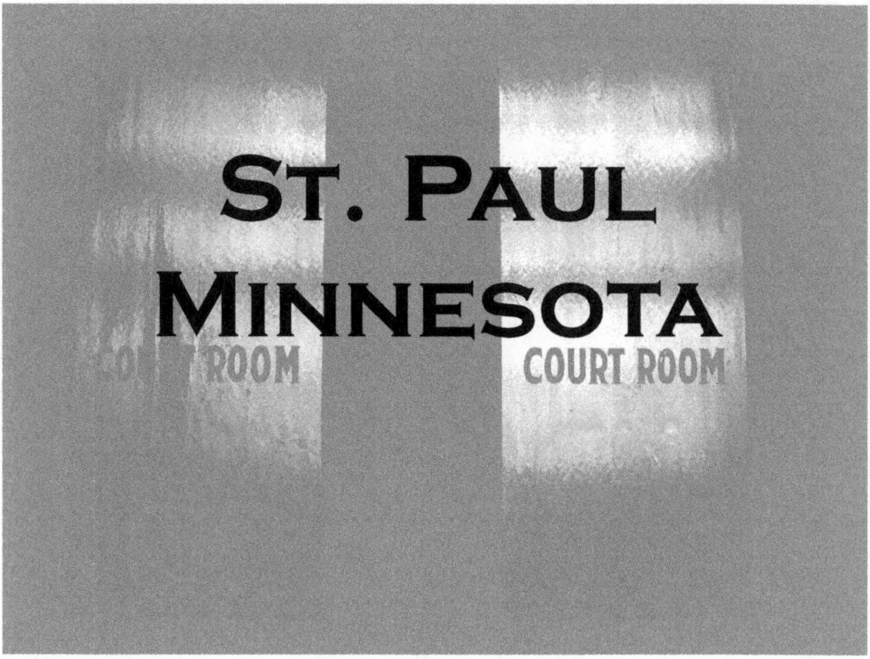

The Wabasha Street Caves

Location:

215 Wabasha St. S

St Paul, MN 55107

(651) 224-1191

www.wabashastreetcaves.com

Directions:

From Kellogg Blvd. turn south on Wabasha St. and pass over the bridge and continue on for several blocks. The caves will be on your right.

Gangster Lore:

Unfortunately in the United States we have a tendency to consider any building that has stood over 20 years as being outdated. It is getting increasing harder and harder to find an establishment that maintains some semblance of history and character. Luckily for you, the Wabasha Street Caves is one such place. From the minute you walk in to the elegant ballroom you are transported back in time, you can almost hear Cab Calloway and his band playing as you slowly drift back to the 1930s. However, you might not want to get too comfortable at the caves, as this was a favorite hangout of the country's most infamous gangsters, which meant that if you made one wrong move, it would have been your last.

History:

Early 1900s – The caves started out as a mushroom producing farm, and quickly became the largest producer of mushrooms in the United States. The caves were also plentiful with silica, and much of it was mined out and sold to make glass for the booming expansion of the automobile.

1900s – The caves were used to house a speakeasy called the Wabasha Street Speakeasy, and the main whiskey still was operated in cave number seven.

1932 – William and Josie Lehmann began the process of turning the caves into a legal nightclub.

1933 – The caves legally re-opened and celebrated the grand opening of the Castle Royal nightclub.

1941 – The nightclub closed during the down time of World War II. The caves reverted back to producing mushrooms as a source of income.

1965 – The Lehmann family sold the property.

1972 – Looking to turn the caves back into a nightclub, the property was once again renovated. A nightclub called the Castle Royal 2 opened as a disco inside the caves.

Currently – The caves are used as a dance hall and wedding facility, along with offering weekly guided tours and a Wednesday swing night.

Investigation:
The fun and excitement of the Wabasha Street speakeasy meant that many of the most infamous underworld characters spent their nights dancing, drinking, and plotting new crimes while inside the luxury of the caves. The caves were a grand central station for gangsters spending time in Minnesota. On any given night the general public could mingle with the deadliest gangsters in the country. The caves served as a favorite meeting spot

for Arthur "Doc" Barker and his brother Fred, in addition to several other members of the Barker Gang, including the mastermind behind their crimes, Alvin "Creepy" Karpis. Even Baby Face Nelson was said to enjoy the terrific nightlife provided by the speakeasy.

One of the main legends circulating about the street caves tells of a deadly card game that took place during 1934. Four unsavory looking men were gathered around a card table playing a high-stakes game of poker. Curiously, all of the men were known to carry large music cases with them, even though not one of them was a musician. Sometime during the game a heated argument broke out. Soon the cleaning lady was startled by the sounds of machine gun fire. As she rushed in to see what he happened she was greeted by the sight of three dead bodies lying in a quickly expanding pool of blood on the floor. The woman noticed that the fourth man was still alive and uninjured. Immediately, the St. Paul Police were called in to investigate the crime. Upon arrival, the police told the scared young woman not to worry about anything, they would take care of everything. When the woman came back to see if the police were finished, the dead bodies were mysteriously gone, and the place had been scrubbed completely clean. The police told her that she might want to go home and get some rest, because she had obviously imagined the whole thing. They also told her that she had better not waste their time again with these foolish false alarms.

Even though the police had questioned the sanity of the woman, she had proof, physical proof that you can see today, because if you look closely above the fireplace, you can still observe the bullet holes from the deadly card game.

I spoke with a tour guide at the caves who shared with me a story of an event that was said to have taken place in the caves during 1934. The story goes that three young women were attending a soiree at the club, when a handsome gentleman approached one of them and politely asked her to dance. It was the 1930s, and being that she did not know the gentleman, she normally would have declined the stranger's offer. Yet there was something about the man's confidence and brashness that compelled the young woman to accept. When the song ended, the stranger thanked her for the dance, and proceeded to leave the club with a few of his friends. Immediately, a fellow club patron came rushing up to the

woman and asked her if she had any idea who she had just danced with. When she replied that she had absolutely no idea who her dance partner was, the man said, "that was John Dillinger." This is a wonderful story, but is it credible? Skeptics claim that there is no positive proof that Dillinger actually visited the street caves. However, it should be noted that like most other gangster hot spots around the U.S., the owners did not exactly advertise in the paper that wanted criminals were sheltered at their places. While no absolute proof links Dillinger to the speakeasy, on many occasions guests remembered spotting Homer Van Meter inside the caves. The fact that Van Meter, one of Dillinger closet friends and associates, repeatedly visited the caves lends credibility to the legend of Dillinger dancing the night away at the Wabasha Street Caves.

Tommy Gun Adventures:
Relive the splendor of the big band era each Wednesday as the caves host an open swing dance night. Or, if dancing is not your favorite activity, you can take a guided tour of the caves every Saturday and Sunday.

St. Paul Hotel (Hotel St. Paul)

Location:

350 Market Street (Formerly 363 St. Peter Street)

St. Paul, MN 55102

(651) 292-9292

www.saintpaulhotel.com

Directions:

From Downtown head west on Kellogg Blvd. Turn north on
Market Street and the hotel will be on your right.

Gangster Lore:

It is said that without Prohibition people like Al Capone and
Leon Gleckman would not have risen to the levels of power and

prominence that they did. Prohibition provided these ambitious bootleggers with the ability to gain unlimited wealth, while they enjoyed a certain prestige among many of the country's working class citizens. While Capone was using his unique form of persuasion to run things in down in Chicago, St. Paul's illegal liquor was being taken care of by Leon Gleckman. With money being no object, Leon decided to turn the third floor of the Hotel St. Paul into his personal bootlegging and criminal headquarters, where he conducted business, took payoffs, and attracted the attention of the Federal Government.

History:

1856 – Local entrepreneur John Summers welcomed travelers from around the country to come and stay at his lovely home in St. Paul.

1871 – Looking to expand on his business, Mr. Summers constructed the Greenman House which operated as a 60-room hotel.

1878 – A major fire roared through the hotel and the Greenman House was completely destroyed.

1878 – Mr. Summers was anxious to re-build his business so he took on John Baugh as his new partner. Together the two men drew up plans to build a brand new hotel. The new hotel was designed to be much larger and more modern than the Greenman House. The men decided to call their new hotel "The Windsor."

1880 – Soon Baugh found himself tiring of the hotel business and decided to get out of the partnership. Baugh sold his stake in the Windsor Hotel to a Mr. Charles J. Monfort.

1891 – Mr. Summers resigned from the company he helped start, leaving Mr. Monfort with the sole responsibility of running the business.

1904 – Charles Monfort passed away.

1904-1906 – Suffering from some hard times, the hotel operated as a theater and an arcade.

1908 – Lucius Ordway purchased the property. Mr. Ordway held the lofty goal of creating a new luxury hotel in St. Paul.

1910 – After much planning the Hotel St. Paul celebrated its grand opening with a large and elegant ceremony. The hotel was

known far and wide as "St. Paul's Million Dollar Hotel."

1930 – Gangster Leon Gleckman rented out several rooms on the third floor. To keep an eye on Gleckman the Federal Govern-

ment also rented a room at the hotel.

1950s – Due to years of neglect and lack of upkeep, the dilapidated hotel was in a sorry state of condition.

1982 – The St. Paul business community realized the importance of the hotel, and began an arduous process to save it. A monstrous renovation project began that hoped to restore the 254-room hotel to its original grandeur.

1983 – Because of the complete renovation of the building, the address of the hotel was changed from St. Peter Street to Market

Street.

Currently – The upscale hotel is open to the public.

Source: St. Paul Hotel

Investigation:

The Hotel St. Paul was a popular place for gangsters to hang out and conduct their underworld business. It got to be so popular that the authorities considered it a major hot spot for illegal activity. Eventually the gangster hangout ushered in so much illegal activity that the Feds considered it a prime location to keep tabs on what the Twin Cities underworld was up to. One of their main targets was Leon Gleckman, who was dubbed "the Al Capone of St. Paul." If a major crime occurred in the Twin Cities, you could bet that Gleckman had his hand in it. At one point in time Gleckman was overseeing nearly all of the illegal liquor traffic that was going in and out of St. Paul.

To help cement his position, and his pocketbooks, Gleckman often used his powerful political connections to gain favors for others in the city, thus providing him with a piece of the profit from many different illegal operations. In 1922, Gleckman was arrested by Prohibition agents who discovered that he was operating 13 stills in his business. The *Brainerd Daily Dispatch* reported that Gleckman, like any good gangster, tried to bribe the jury for his release. After being sentenced to 18 months in prison, he quietly served his time, and was subsequently released. With his stint in prison falling to rehabilitate him, Gleckman immediately got back into his old habits, and soon set up shop on the third floor of the Hotel St. Paul. At the hotel he transformed rooms 301-303 into his personal offices. While staying at the hotel Gleckman used the rooms to oversee his various business enterprises and to conduct business with underworld contacts from all over the United States. It should be noted that the third floor was not the only section of the hotel where illegal dealings transpired, as the extensive lobby provided the perfect convenient meeting place for many busy gangsters. Researcher Paul Maccabee wrote that the lobby of the hotel was at the heart of illegal dealings. It was in the lobby where Gleckman's men collected weekly payments from the Hollyhocks Club, and an assortment of other various establishments that paid a percentage of their profits to Gleckman.

Of course, all of the illegal activity transpiring at the hotel finally attracted the attention of the Federal Government. The St. Paul Hotel staff informed me that during the 1930s, the FBI rented out room 309. A bit smaller that the other rooms, room 309 was used to keep constant surveillance on Gleckman along with the constant parade of gangsters coming in and out of the place. The end of Prohibition presented Gleckman with a new career opportunity. Now that the bootlegging money had dried up, Gleckman decided to trade his illegal professional in for a more respected run at politics. Gleckman did not experience some transformative epiphany where he suddenly saw the value of public service, instead he figured that he could easily capitalize on all of his powerful connections and earn more money from illegally secured contracts that he ever could from making booze. In 1941, with an impending prison sentence waiting for him, Gleckman crashed his car in St. Paul, an accident that took his life. However, many speculated that Gleckman's death was no mere accident, in the end it was said that instead of going back to prison, Gleckman chose death.

Tommy Gun Adventures:
The St. Paul Hotel staff informed me that due to several major renovations at the hotel, rooms 301-303 are not set up the same as they were in the 1930s, yet you still can rent out a room that was part of 301-303. Of course, you can also hang out in the hotel lobby and hope that a passing gangster will drop off the weekly payment.

Old St. Paul Police Headquarters
(Currently the Public Safety Building)

Location:

100 East 11th Street (Formerly 101 E. 10th Street)

St. Paul, MN 55101

Directions:

The Public Safety Building is located in downtown St. Paul on 11th Street, which runs parallel to Interstate 94. The building is located between N. Robert Street and Minnesota Street N.

Gangster Lore:

Gangsters and police officers seem to go hand-in-hand or, I

should say, hand-in-hand-cuff. But these groups were not always on different sides of the law, at least not officially. Back in the ol' days of St. Paul the police employed a more liberal approach in their dealings with the so-called bad guys. Many police officers thought that instead of spending their limited time and money on trying to capture the gangsters, it might be more beneficial if they allowed the gangsters to roam freely in exchange for a generous donation. One such place where these under-the-table deals were struck was the St. Paul Police Headquarters. But beware... this is still a functioning city building and the St. Paul Fire Department is housed here, so those of you who are "on the lam" right now may want to postpone visiting this location.

History:

1900 – John O'Connor was made St. Paul's Chief of Police.

1912 – Chief O'Connor resigned claiming that he wanted to pursue other business opportunities.

1912 – Martin J. Flanagan was positioned as the new acting police chief.

1914 – The popular John O'Connor once again became the St. Paul Police Chief.

1920 – Wanting to enjoy more time away from work, O'Connor resigned for the final time as St. Paul Police Chief.

1921 – Henry J. Crepeau was appointed to replace Chief O'Connor.

1922 – Frank W. Sommers served as the St. Paul Police Chief.

1924 – John O'Connor passed away from ill health at the age of sixty-eight.

1924 – Edward J. Murnane served as the St. Paul Police Chief.

1929 – A contract for the construction of a new police headquarters building was issued and construction on the Roman-Dorie style building began.

1932 – Thomas E. Dahill served as the St. Paul Police Chief.

1934 – Michael J. Culligan served as the St. Paul Police Chief. Chief Culligan was the last chief to uphold the O'Connor system. He upheld the tradition until his suspension.

1930 – The new police headquarters building was completed.

1935 – In a massive investigation into corruption, phone taps were installed inside the police station. The investigation turned up scores of corrupt cops.

1958 – The city Health Department moved out of the building to a new location on Cedar Street.

1985 – The police headquarters was moved to a new location on Grove Street.

1985 – The building was completely gutted. During the renovation, the main entrance was moved to 100 East Eleventh Street. The design was kept similar to the look of the building in the 1930s. The renovated building was named the James S. Griffin Building, in honor of the deceased deputy chief, who was the first African American to achieve a high rank in the police department.

Currently – The building houses the St. Paul Fire Department.

Investigation:

In 1935, the *United Press* wrote, "No city ever enjoyed a greater immunity from crime than St. Paul under the iron fist of Police Chief John J. O'Connor." Thanks to Chief O'Connor, if you were a gangster from anywhere in the United States, you could find a safe place to "cool off" in St. Paul. Of course, you first had to abide by what became known as the O'Connor System. The O'-Connor System was really quite simple. Upon entering the Twin Cities, the gangster would venture down to the police station to check in with officials. Once you had registered with the police, you were practically free to do as you wished. You could rob a bank, gun down a rival, and/or commit an assortment of nearly any other crimes, and the St. Paul Police would not do a thing about it. However, this too good to be true scenario did come with one small catch-----you couldn't commit these crimes in St. Paul. What that meant was that you could go over to Minneapolis, or any other city, and shoot up their banks, kill their gangsters, or kidnap someone, but there would be no crime in the city of St. Paul. Yet, saying that there was "no" crime in St. Paul is a bit of an exaggeration, as certain types of crimes were more than allowed to flourish in the city. The police force had no problem taking protection and kickback money from the numerous brothel owners, bookies, gambling houses, and speakeasies. Not only did this payment prevent you from most police harassment, it also provided you with advance warning if any honest police or feds were about to raid your home or establishment.

The O'Connor System and the idea of St. Paul being a safe haven for criminals stemmed from John O'Connor's truly unique perspective on crime. O'Connor felt that as long as the unsavory characters staying in St. Paul behaved themselves, the police force would pretty much leave them alone. The *Oelwein Daily Register* wrote that O'Connor used to tell crooks to "live, spend and have a good time here, but if you play any tricks here you'll spend the rest of your life in jail." If any criminals were foolish enough not to adhere to the deal, they quickly found out that it was much better to be on the good side of O'Connor, than to be on his bad side. This intricate policing system seemed to work out splendidly for St. Paul, as local newspaper and pamphlets of the time proudly touted that the safety of the residents of St. Paul, and the virtue of the women was assured. Chief O'Connor retired from the police force in 1912. He had stated that he was leaving because he wanted to pursue other business opportunities. However, a change in leadership would not be felt as by this time the police and criminals were so entrenched in the O'-Connor System that things simply continued as though nothing had changed. Two years later, O'Connor would be persuaded to once again serve the people of St. Paul as their Police Chief. O'Connor served as chief until 1920, when he permanently re-signed from the force.

A real testament to the power of the O'Connor System came from its long duration. After O'Connor retired in 1920, his system seemed to only flourish and grow over the establishment and reign of the next six police chiefs. However, the atypical system set up by O'Connor could not last forever, and when St. Paul residents finally got fed up with their city being the gangster capital, they called on their officials to clean up the city from corruption. Starting in 1934, 27-year-old Chicago criminologist, Wallace Jamie, led a secret investigation into police corruption in St. Paul. Jamie had wiretaps installed into police telephones, offices, and hallways, in hopes of discovering the extent of the corruption. During the year-long investigation, Jamie had taped over 2,500 telephone conversations in which police officers were captured soliciting bribes, protecting illegal gambling rings, and tipping off wanted gangsters. Needless to say, Jamie's findings did nothing to diminish St. Paul's reputation of being the gangster capitol of the United States. In the fallout from the federal investigation, newspapers around the country ran scintillating stories of the police corruption in St. Paul. A June 27 article in the *La Crosse Tribune* reported that Inspector James Crumley, and Detectives Fred Raasch, Ray Flannagan, and Michael McGinnis were being charged with "soliciting and accepting bribes and failing to detect and suppress crime." The public backlash was so great that even Police Chief Michael J. Culligan was handed a 30-day suspension. Not looking to go out without a fight, the chief issued a statement that many newspapers, including the *La Crosse Tribune*, stating, "No person has or can say a single word against my honesty." Eventually, when the fervor settled down and all was said and done, Chief Culligan did resign. Perhaps even more troubling for the corrupt officers was the announcement from the IRS that they would immediately begin an investigation into the income tax records of all persons involved in the case. At the completion, the investigation had complied over 3,000 pages of evidence linking numerous police officers with the city's rogue gangsters. After the damaging investigation, the end of Prohibition, and the continued pressure and help from the FBI, St. Paul began to regain some of its credibility among the citizens, and the city's sinister gangster past was slowly forgotten by many...until now.

The Infamous Hollyhocks Club and Casino

Location:

1590 South Mississippi River Blvd.

St. Paul, MN 55116

Directions: *Private Residence – View from road*

Take Highway 5 west and take the Edgcumbe Ave./ Shepard Rd. exit and continue to Shepard Rd. Take a right on Shepard Rd and follow it to S Mississippi River Blvd. The large white home is located between 1616 and 1606 S Mississippi River Blvd. as the homes are not numbered in sequential order.

Gangster Lore:

During the early 1920s and 30s the Twin Cities were flush with speakeasies, dance halls, brothels, and illegal gambling rooms. Filled with big band music, gourmet meals, and of course illegal spirits, these establishments often gained a reputation as the places to see and be seen. Yet none of these places could match the infamy of the Hollyhocks Club. At the secluded Hollyhocks, politically powerful and well-to-do customers could eat, drink, dance, gamble, and mingle side-by-side with some of the most wanted criminals in America.

History:

1904 – The vacant land was purchased by Henry and Cornelia Boardman, who constructed their family home on the land.

1929 – Harry Silver and Walter McKenna purchased the mansion with plans to open it as a gambling hall and restaurant.

1931 – Known gangster Jack Peifer bought out McKenna's half of the operation. The name of the club was changed to Hollyhocks in honor of the wild plant that was growing all over the property.

1932 – Due to the mounting pressure to rid the country of crime, the Hollyhocks Club was placed under surveillance by the Feds. Phone taps were installed, customers were followed, and even the Hollyhocks' mail was tampered with.

1934 – The FBI recorded dozens of phone calls between gangsters and corrupt police officers. The political and police pressure became so regular that the Hollyhocks Club officially closed down.

Currently – The building is used as a private residence.

Source: John Dillinger Slept Here

Investigation:
Much of what is known about the Hollyhocks Club comes from the detailed research of Paul Maccabee who wrote about the club in his brilliant book, *John Dillinger Slept Here*.

The three-story building functioned as both a supper club and casino that catered to the Twin Cities' wealthy and elite. The first floor of the building housed a large, elegant kitchen where Japanese waiters served exquisite meals for the upscale patrons.

This floor also contained a large dance floor, private dining areas, and a fully stocked bar. The second floor of the building was comprised of the main gambling room, where after dinner guests could try their luck at several rigged games including craps, roulette, and black jack. The gambling room brought in much of the Hollyhocks' profit. The third floor of the home contained the private bedroom of Jack Peifer, and had several additional sleeping rooms for VIP guests. Like most of the criminal activity in St. Paul, in order for the casino to operate without police harassment, a deal had been arranged for the casino to "donate" a portion of their profits to the police and politicians in exchange for protection from prosecution. Long time bank robber Eddie Bentz provided some details on this arrangement when interviewed by the *San Antonio Light*, stating, "When Leon Gleckman had St. Paul, and Jack Peifer was running the Holly Hocks Inn, all a fellow had to do was to take care of Jack. In my own case, I never bothered to find out where the dough went after I saw Jack. He looked after all the details."

In addition to its traditional role as a restaurant and casino, the Hollyhocks also provided a safe meeting place for gangsters to plan and organize future crimes with their colleagues. Numerous gangsters frequented the establishment including the Barker-Karpis gang, Harry Sawyer, Vern Miller, Fred "Shotgun George Ziegler" Goetz, Homer Van Meter, and various other underworld operators. It was also inside the walls of the Hollyhocks during 1933 that Jack Peifer met with Alvin Karpis and Fred Barker to propose his plan of kidnapping the Hamm's Brewing heir

William Hamm. It was Peifer's belief that Hamm could be successfully held for a ransom of $100,000. However, with all of the suspicious activity taking place at the Hollyhocks, it was only a matter of time before the attention of the FBI was focused on the club. For the most part, the payoff money to local officials had no bearing on Federal Agents. In 1932, the authorities put the club under surveillance and began tapping the phone lines. What they discovered was that the club functioned more or less as a ground zero for criminal communication throughout the entire country. In 1934, amid political pressure, and Jack Peifer's legal troubles, the Hollyhocks Club was officially closed down and another chapter in St. Paul's illegal past was forever closed.

America's First Car Bombing
The Death of Dapper Dan

Location:

1607 West Seventh Street

St. Paul, MN 55102

Currently: A private residence-- view from the road. Alleyway behind house is open to the public.

Directions:

Take Highway 5 to the west. Immediately after passing house number 1607, turn right on May Street. Drive half a block and you will see the alleyway on the right.

Gangster Lore:

It was said that "Dapper" Dan Hogan was quite the character. A large and gregarious man Hogan earned his well-deserved moniker from always being dressed to the nines. But underneath his flashy expensive tailor-made suits Hogan was a well-connected negotiator in the St. Paul underground. Researchers believe that Hogan had just as much pull and power at the police station as he did with the unsavory characters of the Twin Cities. He was a man that was both respected and feared among the legal, and not so legal players around town. So how could a man dubbed by the underworld as "The Smiling Peacemaker" fall victim to such a violent end? The simple answer is that we don't know, as the case was never officially solved. However, those of you who are aspiring detectives should have no trouble solving this case.

History:

1905 –As a young man Dan Hogan spent time in San Quentin prison.

1909 – After prison Hogan arrived in Minnesota and quickly set up shop in St. Paul.

1927 – Officials indicted Hogan for conspiracy to commit a 1924 St. Paul robbery.

1928 – Dapper Dan Hogan died from injuries caused by a bomb planted under his car.

Investigation:

On the morning of December 4, 1928, Dapper Dan leisurely strolled out to his coupe not knowing that death was there waiting for him. Underneath his car a bomb had been rigged up to the vehicle's starter. As soon as Hogan fired up the car, he was rocked back by the incredible force of the bomb. Paul Maccabee wrote in *John Dillinger Slept Here*, that the bomb blast was so powerful that it shot Dan's car out from the garage into the alley. The bomb was so powerful that it blew a large hole in the roof, blew out the windows, and tore the steering wheel completely from its post. The bomb had done quite a number on Hogan as well. According to Erik Rivenes' audio tour *St. Paul's Most Notorious*, the only thing that kept Hogan from immediate death was the position of his seat. Hogan was a large and round man, and in order to fit into the car, the seat needed to be adjusted and positioned further back to accommodate his girth. Therefore the blast did not hit Hogan with its full impact, which would have certainly caused his immediate death. After the explosion Dan was rushed to the hospital where doctors frantically tried to save his life. The *Port Arthur* wrote that in their pursuit to save him, doctors amputated his right leg which had been completely "shattered" by the bomb. Curiously, the newspapers stated that Hogan went against his doctors recommendations and refused any anesthetic. Of course if you were in the business of keeping secrets, and planned to survive the surgery, you too might have skipped any chance of divulging information while on painkillers. Hogan told Edward Diehl, Assistant Ramsey County Attorney, "I don't know what happened or why it happened."

Hogan was also heard telling doctors, "I touched the starter and that's all I remember. I don't know who could have done it. I didn't know I had an enemy in the world." News of the bombing spread and dozens of friends and citizens came forward offering the underworld boss their blood for a transfusion. However, their actions proved futile as Hogan's injuries were just too severe, and shortly before 9 p.m. he died.

Newspapers around the country quickly speculated on who was behind the risky gangland bombing. The December 5 edition of the *Oelwein Daily Register* wrote that "Police worked the theory that Minneapolis gamblers had imported New York gangsters to put an end to Hogan." If Hogan knew who was behind the attack, he did not let on, as the *Murphysboro Daily Independent* wrote that "Hogan, always tight lipped, died without naming the enemies he perhaps knew were responsible for the dynamite plant." The official police version is that they did not know who was responsible for the death of Hogan. Yet, it is much more plausible that the police knew who was behind the bombing, but had other motives guiding their investigation. Dan's wife told St. Paul newspapers that early that same morning she had noticed two men stop near the garage. Not being able to recognize the men, Mrs. Hogan went about her business as usual. It is believed that those two men she had spotted snuck into the garage and placed the bomb under Hogan's car. Whoever was responsible evidently knew Hogan's habit's pretty well, as the other car parked in the garage was left untouched. Although the case was never officially solved, rumors circulated throughout the area that the

bomb was the handiwork of Hogan's trusted employee Harry
Sawyer. After the death of her husband, Mrs. Hogan went to
clear out a secret safe deposit box containing over $50,000.
However, when she got to the bank, the box was empty. The
only other person that knew of its existence was Harry Sawyer,
who after Hogan's death also took control of the Green Lantern
Saloon and, of course, all the profitable deals that came with it.
Sawyer would meet his own death in 1955 after being released
from prison with dire medical conditions.

Tommy Gun Adventures:
You can still see where America's first car bombing took place.
Drive or walk by Dan's former home, and take a stroll through
the alleyway where Dan met his fate.

Ma Barker and the Barker Gang Hideout

Location:

1031 South Robert Street

St Paul, MN 55118

(Private residence – please view from road)

Directions:

From Highway 52, turn west on Butler Ave. E. Follow Butler to Robert Street S. and turn north. The house will be on your left.

Gangster Lore:

Perhaps the greatest general public misnomer of the history of gangsters is the popular belief that Kate "Ma" Barker was the mastermind criminal that forced her sons into a lifetime of crime.

In this case the legend could not be further from the truth, as contrary to popular belief it was actually the outlaw Barker boys who thought that traveling with their innocent looking mother would create less suspicion. The Barkers were some of the deadliest set of criminals of their time, and having Ma Barker along for cover allowed them to blend in among normal everyday people. Of course the idea of a gun tooting southern woman blindly protecting her children is a hard misconception to break. But as you will soon see, it was her boys' criminal behavior that dragged the caring Ma Barker on a journey of robberies, kidnappings, and shootings that would eventually get her and her sons killed.

History:

1873-1874 – Arizona Clark was born in Missouri. Although most researchers believe that Arizona Clark was born in 1873 or 1874, the birth date on her tombstone is listed as 1877.

1892 – Arizona Clark married George Elias Barker and became known as Kate Barker.

1894 – The couple had their first child, a baby boy named Herman Barker.

1896 – Lloyd Barker was the second son to be born.

1899 – Arthur "Doc" Barker was born.

1902 – Fred Barker was born. Fred was the last of the Barker children.

1918 – Doc Barker was convicted of killing a night watchman at St. John's Hospital during a drug theft that went wrong.

1927 – While robbing a store in Kansas, Herman Barker was wounded by police. During the robbery Herman shot and killed policeman J. E. Marshall, but before the police could capture him, Herman took his own life with his Luger pistol.

1932 – Lloyd was convicted on charges of mail robbery. He was sentenced to 25 years at the United States Penitentiary in Leavenworth, Kansas.

1932 – Doc Barker was pardoned by Oklahoma Governor William Murray.

1935 – Doc Barker was sentenced to life imprisonment for his role in the kidnapping of Edward Bremer.

1935 – The FBI raided the house that Ma Barker and her son Fred were renting in Ocklawaha, FL. After several hours of gun fighting, Ma and Fred were found dead inside the house. Ma's body had 4 bullets in it, while Fred was filled with 11 bullets.

1935 – Doc Barker was killed while trying to escape from Alcatraz.

1949 – Lloyd Barker was killed by his wife.

Investigation:

Most crime scholars agree that Ma Barker was certainly not the brains behind the Barker crime operation. It is much more plausible that Ma was certainly aware of her sons' criminal activities, but had no direct hand in orchestrating or committing the actual crimes. Ma Barker was gunned down in Florida, and the *Brainerd Daily Dispatch* reported that when agents "burst into the house they found Barker dead and 'Ma' Barker's body nearby with a machine gun in her lifeless fingers." Instead of facing the publicity nightmare of having killed a mostly innocent elderly woman, it was the FBI's job to turn Ma Barker from a loving mother of moderate intelligence (at best) into a controlling ruthless murdering fugitive that showed no regard for human life. FBI Director, J. Edgar Hoover, wasted no time in setting forth a campaign to re-shape the public perception of Ma Barker. Hoover created such a masterly spun smear campaign that the image of Ma Barker as a dangerous outlaw successfully lives on even to this day. Yet even if Ma Barker wasn't a death causing criminal, her sons more than made up for her innocence. Those who knew the family felt that the boys were simply destined for a life of crime. From an early age the boys were so adept at getting in trouble with the law that one could easily argue that criminal behavior was an innate Barker trait. Of course this appetite for lawbreaking acted like a giant magnet, attracting them to the City of St. Paul.

While in St. Paul the Barker family was renting a home on
Robert Street from a Mrs. Hannegraf, under the alias of the An-
dersons. Ma Barker, and her boyfriend, Arthur Dunlop, were pos-
ing as Mr. and Mrs. George Anderson, while Fred Barker and
Alvin "Creepy" Karpis were claiming to be musicians. The
group even carried around violin cases to help with the deception. It was in this modest home that the Barker gang set about
planning for the robbery of the Northwestern National Bank in

Minneapolis.

On March 29, the gang's detailed planning paid off as the gang
successfully robbed the bank of over $75,000 in cash, $6,000 in
coin, and nearly $190,000 in bonds. After the robbery the group
retreated to the safety of their Robert Street home to count up

and divide their newly acquired loot. For a while everything seemed to be going right for the cash flush gang. After years of struggle the gang had finally secured the wealth and notoriety that came along with a sting of high profile robberies. The cold blooded killers were even highly regarded neighbors. Researcher Paul Maccabee wrote that the gang was often described by neighbors as extremely nice people, so likeable in fact that they even drove Mrs. Hannegraf's granddaughter to Catholic School. But like all gangsters, their luck was about to take a turn for the worse. The friendly landlady who lived right next to the house they rented had a son that owned Drover's Tavern. One evening while closing up the bar, Mrs. Hannegraf's son, Nick, decided to catch up on some light reading and grabbed a copy of True Detective magazine. As Nick leisurely flipped through the pages, he immediately recognized that several of the "musicians" who were renting his mother's home were actually wanted men with $100 rewards attached to them. Wound up by his amazing discovery, the son rushed to his mother's house in the middle of the night to share his big news. Nick quietly woke his mother up and showed her the wanted posters from the crime magazine. Without hesitation Mrs. Hannegraf also identified the wanted men as her friendly neighbors. While Mrs. Hannegraf was stealthily crawling through the garage writing down the gang's license plate numbers, Nick was speeding off to the police station to collect the reward. Once Nick reached the police station he could hardly contain his prized information. Nick approached the first person he saw and blurted out that Fred Barker and Alvin Karpis were asleep in the home next to his mother. Needless to say Nick's information was not greeted with the enthusiasm he had anticipated. In fact, from the very moment he walked into the station, Nick was witness to the power of the corrupt O'Connor System. The unmotivated police officer initially accused Nick of being drunk. Trying to plead his case, Nick showed the officer his copy of True Detective magazine. After taking a cursory glance at the magazine the officer put Nick into a Waiting room and informed him that they would be back to get his full statement. Meanwhile, several calls were placed and the Barker gang was tipped off that their cover had been blown. By the time the police actually got to the rented home, the gang was long gone. In their hastily escape they had left behind many personal items that confirmed their identity.

Unfortunately for Arthur Dunlop (Ma Barker's boyfriend), the gang believed that it was his loose mouth, not the True Detective magazine, that led to their discovery. Perhaps others would have let the mistake go with a only harsh warning, but the Barkers were not a very forgiving bunch. On May 1, 1932, the *Wisconsin State Journal* reported that "Dunlop's bullet riddled and naked body was found at Fremstad Lake near Webster, Wis." With Dunlop "removed" from the picture, the gang continued on their crime spree of Minnesota, but their luck could not run on forever.

Within a just couple years of Dunlop's death, Ma and Fred would met their end as well. On January 16, 1934 after a long and successful crime spree spanning many years, Ma Barker and her son

Fred were hiding out in their Lake Weir rental house in FL. Little did the two know that 15 law enforcement agents had surrounded the place. The agents shouted out for the Barker's to surrender, and according to the *Key West Citizen*, the agents were answered with "a blaze of machine gun fire." A fierce gun battle ensued in which the agents riddled the home with thousands of bullets. Shortly after the initial gunfire the house fell eerily silent. Convinced that the Barker's were setting a trap the agents cautiously waited for any sign of life. Inside the home Fred and his mother were dead, but the authorities did not know this yet, so every time the curtain blew in the wind the agents opened fired on the house. Finally after six hours of firing at the wind the cautious agents sent the Barker's hired cook to check out the situation. Once inside, the cook discovered the dead bodies of Fred and Ma and the gunfight was over.

Tommy Gun Adventures:
Although the old Barker gang's rented house is currently a private residence, when you walk by you can almost sense the Barker gang still inside counting up their stolen money. Of course, you can also drive in the alleyway behind the house and recreate the gang's early morning escape.

Como Park Zoo Killing

Location:

Como Park and Zoo

1225 Estabrook Drive

Saint Paul, MN 55103

Directions:

The Barker-Karpis gang pulled over to switch cars in the area surrounding Monkey Island, which is now Seal Island. Follow Lexington Parkway until Estabrook Drive, and you can make a circle around the area. You can also enter the zoo (for free) and walk around the area where the actually murder took place.

Gangster Lore:

For years, people have traveled to St. Paul to enjoy the beauty and charm of Como Park and Zoo. Visitors are drawn to the tranquil surroundings of the rolling green acres of the expansive park. On many occasions the park functions as a picnic area, recreation field, and even a wedding chapel. Many people visit Como Zoo to catch a glimpse of the numerous animals that roam the grounds. The seclusion of the area also made it a prime spot along the getaway route for the Barker-Karpis gang. Those who were visiting the area on December 16, 1932, would have discovered that vicious animal behavior was not limited to the zoo animals.

History:

1872 – A group of five commissioners were appointed to purchase between 500 and 650 acres of land within a convenient distance of the city of St. Paul.

1873 – The city of St. Paul purchased 300 acres of prime land near the shores of Lake Como at the cost of $100,000. The land was to be designated for a new public park that would be named Como Park.

1877 – After years of inattention and neglect, city funds were allocated to develop the park into a working area to be enjoyed by the general public.

1897 – The first animals to be placed in the zoo were three deer that were given to the city of St. Paul. A fenced area was constructed for the deer to roam.

1900 – The zoo had grown to include foxes, cattle, deer, and elk.

1915 – Lieutenant Governor Thomas Frankson let his private buffalo roam the area near the park.

1904 – Dr. Rudolph Schiffman donated his large and rare collection of Japanese plants and trees, thus starting the first Japanese Garden in St. Paul.

1915 – The Como Park Conservatory opened.

1932 – The brutal murder of a Christmas wreath salesman took place inside the park near Monkey Island.

1974 – The Como Park Conservatory was placed on the National Register of Historic Places.

1982 – Monkey Island, near where the 1932 shooting took place, was deepened and renovated to accommodate the new Seal Island.

2005 – The Visitor Center at Como Park Zoo and Conservatory began offering education classes.

Currently – The park and zoo is open to the public.

Source: Como Zoo

Investigation:

Still fleeing from their raid of the Third Northwestern Bank, the Barker-Karpis gang was having a problem with one of the car's tires. Having been punctured in the shootout, the tire was completely lost somewhere along the getaway route. While chugging along, the gang noticed that the car's radiator had also been pierced by the gunfire. Luckily, the gang had planned for such setbacks and had left another getaway vehicle near Como Park. Riding on three wheels, the gang stalled their car near the west entrance of the park. After a few tries the gang finally got their vehicle running and pulled up to their backup green sedan which was parked near Monkey Island (today Seal Island). The men quickly began transferring their loot into the new car. In order to completely cover their tracks, the gang needed to switch the license plates of the two cars.

As fate would have it, December 16, 1932, was the first day of work for Oscar Erickson and Arthur Zachman. The two friends were excited about the prospect of earning some holiday money by selling Christmas wreaths throughout the neighborhood. The *St. Paul Pioneer Press* spoke with Mrs. Erickson, who on December 17, told the paper, "It was his first day selling wreaths— he's been out of work." As the duo were heading home from a day of selling wreaths they spotted some men working on two cars that were pulled over on the side of the road. When he drove, Oscar made the fatal mistake of slowing down. The passenger, Arthur Zachman told the *St. Paul Pioneer Press*, "As we went by, Oscar took his foot off the gas and we slowed down a little, looking out to see what was happening." The ever watchful Fred Barker noticed the approaching vehicle, and when he saw the oncoming car slow down and look, he mistakenly believed that the driver was trying to read the car's license plate numbers. While it was claimed that Fred Barker told the men to "keep moving or else," the *Ames Daily Tribune-Times* wrote, "Without warning the bandit gang fired on Erickson." With, or without the alleged warning, Fred unleashed a barrage of bullets that tore through the car. Zachman told the *St. Paul Pioneer Press*, "It was all so sudden that I didn't realize at first what had happened." What had happened was that Erickson was struck in the head by the onslaught of Fred's bullets. Zachman went on to tell the *St. Paul Pioneer Press*, "Oscar slumped down in the driver's seat and his foot must have shoved up against the clutch, because the car started to coast." From the passenger side of the car Zachman grabbed his bloody friend and waited until they were out of sight of the shooters. He then moved into the driver's seat and drove down to the University Avenue police station. He quickly ran out to tell the police that his friend was injured. However, luck was obviously not on his side as the first officer he encountered was Al Salinger, who had just heard about the Minneapolis robbery. Thinking that Zachman might have somehow been involved in the robbery, Salinger searched him for a gun. Once everything was sorted out, Erickson was rushed to the

Ancker Hospital (Currently Regions Hospital) in a police ambulance while Zachman was further questioned by police. At the hospital, doctors frantically tried to save Erickson. It turned out that his wounds were too severe, and by the morning he was pronounced dead.

Back at the park the gang had simply abandoned the old wrecked car and headed off to their hideout. Initially the police had no idea how the gang had acquired their new car. The *Bismarck Tribune* wrote, "St. Paul authorities were checking to determine whether the bandits had stopped some motorist in Como Park, seized his automobile and perhaps taken him along as hostage, or if whether the car might have been 'planted' there for possible use by the bandits."

The authorities were also closing in on the history of the abandoned car. According to the *Bismarck Tribune*: "Police said the bandits abandoned automobile was one stolen here nearly a year ago and was the same one used by a gang (Barker-Karpis) last March when the North American branch of the Northwestern National Bank was robbed." No member of Barker-Karpis gang was ever convicted of the crime, and to this day the murder remains as another bloody reminder of St. Paul's deadly history.

Tommy Gun Adventures:
You can take a stroll through the beautiful Como Park and Zoo area. The place where the Barker-Karpis gang stopped to change cars is the area surrounding Seal Island. You can also hop in your

car and follow the route that the victims took to get away. Travel down Lexington Parkway to University Avenue. Turn left on University and follow it to the intersection of St. Albans Street where the police station was located. Follow University farther to the east and you will run into the old Ancker Hospital (Currently Regions Hospital).

SECOND VICTIM OF MILL CITY BANK HOLDUP SUCCUMBS

St. Paul, Minn.—A second victim of a shooting bank robbery gang which escaped with $20,000 in currency from the Third Northwestern National bank in Minneapolis died Saturday from bullet wounds.

A Minneapolis policeman was killed instantly when he drove up to the bank while the bandits were still ransacking the tellers' cages.

Oscar Erickson, 29, St. Paul, died in Ancker hospital at 4:20 a. m. Saturday. He was shot while riding through Como park in St. Paul when he stopped to stare at the gang as they transferred their loot from a stolen automobile to another car. Without warning the bandit gang opened fire on Erickson.

Patrolman Ira Evans, Minneapolis, was killed when the bandits fired a sub-machine gun from the bank building as he stepped from a police squad car. His companion, Leo Gorsky, another Minneapolis policeman, was in a critical condition and a blood transfusion was necessary.

Three men and a woman who tried to buy tickets to Montreal were questioned by Twin City police as suspects but apparently they could give no information about the robbery. It was expected they would be released.

The Foolhardy Kidnapping of William Hamm

Location:

681 E. Minnehaha Avenue

St. Paul, MN 55106

Directions:

Take Highway 61 (Arcade St) south to Minnehaha Ave. Turn right on Minnehaha and follow it to the intersection of Payne Ave. Here you will see the large abandoned buildings of Hamm's Brewery. This is the location where Hamm was kidnapped in 1933, as he was walking across the street.

Gangster Lore:

Many gangsters looked down upon the act of kidnapping. Not only did they consider it beneath them, they also dreaded the inevitable heat that always accompanied the snatching of a high-profile victim. Many gangsters believed that they ought to stick to the relative easiness of robbing banks, running numbers, bootlegging, prostitution, and numerous other money-making operations that functioned under the radar of both the police, and the public. The risks that kidnapping posed far outweighed the possible benefits. However, the Barker-Karpis gang was not your ordinary play it by the book type of criminals. In fact it may have been the taboo of kidnapping that prompted the gang, regardless of the risks, to venture out on their own and partake in a kidnapping. With their minds made it there was no turning back, all they had left to do was find a perfect victim...

History:

1929 – Fred Goetz was one of the suspected gunmen behind the St. Valentine's Day Massacre, where Al Capone sent men dressed as police officers over to a repair garage run by his rival, Bugs Moran. The fake police officers lined the seven men up against the wall and opened fire on them. All of the men were killed, the only survivor was the manager's dog. The dog was so traumatized by the incident that it had to be put to sleep. Bugs himself had escaped the execution due to the fact that while on his way to the garage he spotted the cops going inside, so he simply kept walking and thus survived.

1933 – The Barker-Karpis gang kidnapped William Hamm. Hamm, a 39-year-old bachelor who lived with his mother, was the heir to the Hamm brewing fortune. Being a handsome single millionaire, Hamm was considered one of the most eligible bachelors in Minnesota.

Investigation:

By 1933, the Barker-Karpis gang were all hardened criminals. Nearly all of them had spent the better part of their lives in trouble with the law. Starting out with humble beginnings, the men participated mostly in petty crimes, but as the years passed, the members had progressed into full-fledged murderous bank robbing outlaws. However, when the plan arose to organize a kidnapping, the gang realized they needed some professional expertise. For that they turned to Hollyhocks proprietor Jack Peifer, who called down to Chicago and summoned the assistance of Fred Goetz. As one of Capone's deadliest men, Goetz had just the kind of expertise the gang was desperately seeking. Goetz also brought with him Bryan Bolton, a fellow Chicago criminal, and Goetz's personal bodyguard. Together Goetz and Bolton sat down with Alvin Karpis, Doc Barker, and Fred Barker. During their initial meeting the group decided that they were a bit shorthanded and would need another man to pull off the job, so they brought in Charles Fitzgerald, who was a personal friend of both Harry Sawyer (proprietor of the Green Lantern) and Jack Peifer. According to FBI files on the Barker-Karpis gang, Fitzgerald was a life-long criminal with numerous outlaw skills.

On June 15, 1933, at 12:45 p.m., William Hamm, a member of the Hamm brewing family, was leaving his office to have lunch at his home. As Hamm crossed the street (Corner of Minnehaha and Greenbrier) Charles Fitzgerald approached him and reached out his arm to shake Hamm's hand. With a firm grip placed on the elbow of Hamm, Fitzgerald asked if the man was indeed William Hamm. The gentleman confirmed that he was Mr. Hamm and inquired what business Fitzgerald wanted. At this point Doc Barker walked into the picture and took hold of Hamm's left hand. Meanwhile, Alvin Karpis, who had been waiting patiently in a parked sedan, drove up right next to the men, and Hamm was forced into the back seat. The gangsters immediately pulled a white pillow case over his head and tucked him out of sight. Hamm was told that if he kept quiet everything would work out just fine. With Hamm safely in their possession the gang met up with Fred Goetz and Fred Barker outside of St. Paul. There Hamm was forced to sign a couple of ransom notes that the gang had already typed up. After signing the documents Hamm was transferred to a hideout in Illinois.

The Kidnapping of Edward Bremer

Location:

Corner of Lexington Parkway and Goodrich Avenue
St. Paul, MN

This case is unique in that it includes several locations that you
can visit, all of which were attached to the kidnapping. Although
I am mostly focusing on the location of the actual kidnapping, I
have included the addresses of the various other locations from
this case for you to visit as well.

Directions:

Location of Bremer Kidnapping – Corner of Lexington Parkway
and Goodrich Avenue, St. Paul. The kidnapping took place at the

stop sign on the corner of Lexington Parkway and Goodrich Avenue on the same side of the street as the Lincoln Court Apartments.

Apartment Where Kidnapping was Planned – Apartment #104 in the Kennington building at 565 Portland Avenue, St. Paul.

Summit School—Drop off of Bremer's daughter – 1150 Goodrich Avenue, St. Paul.

Ditching of Bremer's Bloody Car – 1910 Edgecumbe Road, St. Paul.

Gangster Lore:
Over the years many of us have established a typical routine during our daily lives. Whether it is a detailed process of getting ready in the morning or a special nightly ritual, most of us have developed behavior that is often repeated. For the most part these daily routines are positive and help us accomplish some of the endless goals we have designed for ourselves. However, the same cannot be said for Edward Bremer, whose predictable daily routine attracted the attention of the Barker-Karpis gang. Ironically the gangsters had also begun to fall into a negative routine of their own. This routine consisted of kidnapping rich, high-profile men, which they held for ransom. The gang had no idea that their new ill-formed kidnapping routine would ultimately produce such negative consequences.

History:

1933 – The Barker-Karpis gang successfully kidnapped William Hamm. The gangsters ended up receiving a ransom of $100,000.

1934 – The Barker-Karpis gang kidnapped bank president Edward Bremer while he was on his morning drive to work. Bremer was the son of Adolph Bremer, who headed the Jacob Schmidt Brewery Company. Bremer was also the nephew of Otto Bremer, who was a prominent banker and business man with political connections that reached the White House.

Investigation:

After reveling in the monetary success of the William Hamm kidnapping, the Barker-Karpis gang decided it was time to strike again. Nearly six months had passed since the gang secured a $100,000 ransom from Hamm when they decided it was time to set their sights a bit higher. Together in a Portland Avenue apartment Fred Goetz, Alvin Karpis, William Weaver, Harry Campell, Doc and Fred Barker, Volney Davis, and Harry Sawyer discussed their plans to kidnap Edward Bremer. Bremer, a young bank president, also happened to belong to one of the wealthiest families in Minnesota. In preparation of the crime the men kept Bremer under constant surveillance for several weeks, looking to determine the best possible time to kidnap him. What the gang discovered was that Bremer followed a morning routine so precise that you could set your kidnapping watch to it. On the morning of January 17, 1934, Bremer started out on his normal daily routine. His first stop was at the exclusive Summit School on

Goodrich Avenue, where Bremer dropped off his daughter for her classes. From the school Bremer drove off for his job at the bank. Heading down Goodrich Avenue, Bremer slowed to an idle at the stop sign on the corner of Lexington Parkway and Goodrich Avenue. Bremer was watching for traffic when Fred Barker and Harry Campbell drove up and positioned their vehicle in front of Bremer's, blocking his route. At the same time Karpis, Davis and Doc Barker pulled up behind Bremer and boxed his car in.

Realizing that something was not right, Bremer was quickly met by a firearm-wielding man who instructed him not to move. Panicking, Bremer foolishly struggled with the kidnapper until he was finally subdued by a powerful blast to his head from the butt of a gun. With his face covered in blood, Bremer was forcefully shoved down to the floor of his car. From the floor Bremer cautiously watched the men struggle to re-start his car. Amongst all of the commotion the gangsters were unable to locate the starter button which was located on the car's dash. At first Bremer refused to help the men, but with a few more smashes from the butt of the pistol, Bremer decided it would be best to cooperate. During the whole event not one witness noticed anything out of the ordinary. The January 18 edition of the *Minneapolis Star* reported that there were no witnesses to the kidnapping, writing, "So well was the kidnapping planned that police and federal agents have been unable to locate any witnesses and have but a few clues to guide them." With Bremer in hand the gang roared off from the intersection and quickly ditched Bremer's blood-soaked car near a golf course on Edgecumbe Road. On January 19, the *Minneapolis Star* reported that blood had indeed been found in Bremer's car, stating, "Two large splotches and a smeary streak crimsoned the front cushions and floor of the machine." With his family and friends fearing that he had been killed, Bremer was driven off to a safe hideout in Illinois.

Tommy Gun Adventures:

You can follow in the footsteps of the Barker-Karpis gang as they kidnapped Mr. Bremer. Start your adventure at the Kennington building where the plan was originally hatched. Next make your way to Summit School where Bremer dropped off his daughter. From the school you can go to the intersection of Lexington and Goodrich where Bremer was nabbed. You can then finish this tour by checking out the area where Bremer's bloody car was discovered.

Justice Was Served at the Landmark Center

Location:

75 West Fifth Street

Saint Paul, MN 55102

(651) 292-3233

www.landmarkcenter.org

Directions:

From downtown on Kellogg Blvd. turn onto Market Street and follow it until you pass 5th St. W. The Landmark Center will be on your left.

Gangster Lore:

The beautiful Landmark Center in downtown St. Paul was a major hotspot for gangsters. The Landmark became a well-known place for many gangsters including Jack Peifer, Doc Barker, and Alvin Karpis. Even John Dillinger's girlfriend, Billie Frechette, got to know the Landmark building. However, this wasn't a jazz filled speakeasy or friendly gangster hideout, in the early days the Landmark Center was used to house the Federal Courts Building, which made this one place the gangsters would rather have avoided altogether.

History:

1892 – Detailed construction plans began to create the building.

1902 – The Landmark Center was constructed. The main purpose of the building was to serve as the Federal Court House and Post Office for the Midwest.

1902-1960s – The Ramsey County Courtroom served as the trial location for some of the country's most infamous gangsters, including Doc Baker, Alvin Karpis, Jack Peifer, and Billie Frechette.

1936 – Gangster Jack Peifer was tried and convicted on charges of kidnapping. Jack later committed suicide in his Ramsey County jail cell.

1970s – Concerned citizens fueled on restoring the historic building were able to save the Landmark Center from impending destruction. This same devoted group began the arduous process of trying to bring the building back to the glory days of its youth.

1978 – The Landmark Center was designated as a National Historic Monument and was re-opened to the general public.

Currently – The Landmark Center is used for cultural events, concerts, weddings and a host of other community events.

Investigation:
It was in Ramsey County Courtroom #317 that some of the most infamous criminals of the day were tried, including Evelyn "Billie" Frechette, Doc Barker, Jack Peifer, and Alvin Karpis.

Evelyn "Billie" Frechette

The exciting capture of John Dillinger's girlfriend Evelyn "Billie" Frechette, made national headlines. It was May of 1934, and federal agents were hot of the trail of Dillinger. The agents had staked out a place in Chicago called the Tumble Inn. Inside the gangster friendly bar sat Federal Agent Melvin Purvis. At approximately 8 p.m. a woman walked into the bar and stood right next to Purvis. Recognizing the woman as Billie Frechette, Purvis offered her a chair next to him. Frechette politely shook her head no, and continued on with her business. As Dillinger wisely waited in a car parked down the street, federal agents swarmed in and arrested Frechette. Showcasing the skills she had picked up from the gangsters, Frechette tried to lie her way out of the arrest by insisting that she was not the person the feds thought she was. Unpersuaded by her dishonest protests, the feds arrested Frechette and hauled her out to their car. The commotion had alerted the ever vigilant Dillinger who quickly sped off out of the area, once again eluding the agents.

Frechette was arrested on charges of harboring a fugitive, and her case was set for trial in the Ramsey County Courtroom (Room #317) in St. Paul. Throughout the trial Ms. Frechette claimed that for a very long time she had no idea that the man she was traveling with was the notorious outlaw John Dillinger. However, Judge Gunnar H. Nordbye was not buying her story and stated that, "Miss Frechette knew at all times the identity of John Dillinger." Frechette's defense team proclaimed that any statement gathered from Frechette was done so from heavy-handed agents who put her under intense duress. The defense claimed that in an effort to stop the unpleasant interrogation Frechette had told the authorities what she thought they wanted to hear. For once Frechette may have been telling a bit of the truth when she testified that during her interrogation, the agents had repeatedly slapped her and deprived her of food and sleep for two full days. Newspapers around the country ran the stories on the "third-degree treatment" of Frechette including the *Jefferson City Post-Tribune* which wrote that Billie also claimed that she was not given proper access to a lawyer. None of her objections seemed to matter because on May 23, Evelyn Billie Frechette was found guilty by the Federal Court Jury of conspiracy to harbor John Dillinger. Judge Nordbye sentenced her to two years of imprisonment at the women's reformatory in Alderson, West Virginia. The judge also imposed a fine of $1,000. After her conviction, Frechette wrote several articles for *True Confessions magazine*, where she reiterated the fact that she had been forced into making her previous statements and was innocent of all charges. Frechette would never see Dillinger again.

Arthur "Doc" Barker

Arthur "Doc" Barker was a member of the famed Barker-Karpis Gang. In June of 1933, the gang kidnapped Hamm's brewery owner William Hamm and demanded a ransom of $100,000. Researchers believe that the gang actually received much less than the amount demanded, but this did not put a damper on the gang's future kidnapping plans. In 1934, the gang kidnapped millionaire banker Edward Bremer Jr. and held him ransom for

$200,000. These two high profile kidnapping cases thrust the gang into a nationally known group of criminals. In January of 1935, Arthur Barker was captured by federal agents down in Chicago. Barker was transported to St. Paul to stand trial for the kidnapping of Edward Bremer. It was an open and shut case and Barker was quickly found guilty of conspiracy in the kidnapping of Edward G. Bremer. Looking to send a message to any prospective kidnappers, Judge M.M. Joyce sentenced Barker to life imprisonment. The *Emmetsburg Democrat* reported that Judge Joyce told the jury, "By verdicts such as yours, the incentive to kidnap will soon pass." When sentencing Barker the judge went on to say, "Arthur Barker, you have no defense in this case. No one could doubt your guilt. You have had a fair trial. Kidnapping is one crime that the people of this country will not tolerate." In 1939, Doc Barker was shot to death as he attempted to escape from Alcatraz.

Alvin "Creepy" Karpis

In 1936, Alvin Karpis was hanging out in New Orleans where he was scouting out a couple of possible jobs. He had rented a small apartment where he conducted his research. Unknown to Karpis, the authorities had arrested Grace Goldstein, who was a love interest of Karpis. It was only a mater of time before Goldstein gave in to the multiple threats and shady interrogation techniques and provided the agents with the address where Karpis was staying. As Karpis was attempting to get into his car agents swooped in on him. It was said that Karpis surrender peacefully. Karpis alleged that once he was securely restrained by the agents, FBI Director J. Edgar Hoover then stepped out from behind a wall and aided with the arrest. Hoover had taken a lot of flack over the fact that he had never personally arrested anyone. Hoover took this staged opportunity to claim the credit of capturing one of America's most wanted, and most dangerous men, thus silencing his outspoken critics. Karpis was also brought to St. Paul to stand trial in the kidnapping of William Hamm. While inside the Federal Building, Karpis spent a lot of time in the Detention Room (#324). Before his trial even began, newspapers from around the country began running articles discussing the dim prospect of Karpis' ability to mount a defense. The *Daily Messenger* of Canandaigua, NY wrote that over 100 witnesses were already lined up to testify against Karpis. However, all of the news reports were unnecessary, as Alvin Karpis freely admitted his guilt, and pleaded guilty to conspiracy to the kidnapping of William Hamm. Judge M.M. Joyce sentenced Karpis to life imprisonment. Karpis was sent to the dreaded Alcatraz Prison where he spent more time locked up than any other prisoner.

Jack Peifer

Jack Peifer was the owner of the infamous Hollyhocks Club in St. Paul (See Hollyhocks Chapter). Peifer was arrested on the suspicion of kidnapping William Hamm and his bail was set at $100,000. The government accused Jack of being "the finger man," which meant that Jack was the one that had recommended William Hamm as a suitable target. During his trial inside the Landmark Center the government provided overwhelming evidence of Jack's involvement in the planning of the kidnapping. An article in the *Titusville Herald* claimed that Bryon Bolton testified to the court that Peifer received $10,000 for his part in the kidnapping. With the plethora of evidence collected against him, it was not surprising when Peifer was convicted of aiding in the kidnapping and sentenced to 30 years imprisonment. The Mason City Globe-Gazette reported that Peifer took his sentence harder than all of the others. After his sentencing, Peifer was transferred back to the Ramsey County Jail. Inside the cold cell the prospect of spending the rest of his life behind bars set in. Certain that prison life would not suit him, Peifer swallowed some poison tablets and died. The *La Crosse Tribune* and Leader-Press reported Roy C. Heron, the Chief Deputy Ramsey County Coroner, as saying, "The kind of poison taken by Peifer acts very quickly at times." In an odd note to this case, many staff and visitors to the Landmark Center have reported seeing the ghost of Jack Peifer roaming the halls and continuing to operate the elevators, just as he did when he worked as a bellhop.

Tommy Gun Adventures:
Step back into history with a guided tour of the Landmark Center every Thursday and Sunday.

Dillinger's Shootout at the Lincoln Court Apartments

Location:

93 South Lexington Parkway

St. Paul, MN 55105

Directions:

From Summit Ave. W, turn south onto Lexington Parkway S. Once you cross Lincoln Ave. the apartment complex will be on your right.

Gangster Lore:

In today's world many of us live in places where the history has been forgotten due to both time and disinterest. However, with just a little digging one can find an amazing history to just about any place throughout the country. Nowhere is this more evident than at the Lincoln Court Apartments. Situated in a cozy family St. Paul neighborhood, the unassuming apartment complex is full of tenants who are completely unaware of the fundamental role the building played in the history of gangster activity in Minnesota. Of course, those who do know the history of the building may want to stick to using the front door.

History:

1934 – The apartments were the sight of a shootout between John Dillinger, Homer Van Meter, and law enforcement agents.

2009 – The Lincoln Court Apartments are available for rent to the public.

Investigation:

During March of 1934, John Dillinger and Billie Frechette were living in apartment 303 of the Lincoln Court Apartments under the aliases of Mr. and Mrs. Carl Hellman. Dillinger was hiding out in the apartment trying to get some much needed rest and to recover from some recent injuries. Unfortunately, they had rented an apartment that came along with a snooping landlady. The curious lady paid special attention to the Hellmans and found it peculiar that the young couple would only leave the apartment after dark. To make matters even more bizarre, when the couple did leave, they used the back door exclusively. The landlady really got suspicious when the apartment's maintenance man showed up to make a repair and was refused entry in to the apartment. The degree of odd behavior exhibited by Mr. and Mrs. Hellman prompted the landlady to contact an agent at the FBI's St. Paul office. Not willing to overlook any possible lead the FBI took the lady's report seriously. On March 30, the FBI put the apartment under surveillance, hoping to spot anything out of the ordinary. Although the apartment had its shades closed the agents were able to make out a man and woman who were moving around inside. After a few hours of observation the agents returned to their headquarters and reported that everything about the apartment dwellers seemed normal. The sting of previous failed opportunities was still fresh in the FBI's memory, which prompted them to send over some additional agents, just in case. The next day Federal Agent Rufus Coulter and Detective Henry Cummings walked up to apartment 303 and knocked on the door while several other agents were stationed outside cautiously waiting. Billie hesitantly cracked open the door as far the security chain would allow and peeked out, only to be confronted by two unknown men standing in the hallway. The men asked if they could speak with Carl Hellman. Billie, apparently forgetting her alias, replied, "Carl who?" The men replied "Carl Hellman." Perhaps aware of her slight blunder, Billie told the men that her husband had just left, and that he was not expected to return until later that afternoon and asked if the men could return then to speak with him. Detective Cummings quickly asked Billie if she was Mrs. Hellman, to which she nodded. Not willing to give up so easily the men asked if they could speak with her. Having regained her composure, Billie shyly told the men that she was not properly dressed, and again requested that they return later in the afternoon. The agents, now sensing that something was off, stated that they would be happy wait while she got dressed.

At this point Billie had no choice but to comply with their request. Stalling, Billie explained to the agents that it would take a few minutes for her to get ready as she shut and securely locked the door. Back inside the apartment the ever cool Dillinger told her to calm down and instructed her to gather up some clothes and her bag as the two of them were getting out of there. After waiting for several minutes the lawmen began to sense the ruse, which sent Coulter running off down to the manager's office to call for backup.

While all the drama was transpiring inside the apartment, a suspicious vehicle had stopped outside of the Lincoln Apartments. The agents anxiously watched as an unidentified man (Homer Van Meter) got out of his car and walked into the building heading towards apartment 303. As soon as Van Meter spotted the lawmen standing outside of the apartment, he knew something was wrong, so he tucked his head down and passed right by the men and headed toward the stairwell. As Van Meter was heading down the stairs, Coulter asked him what his name was, and without missing a beat Van Meter replied that he was a just a soap salesman. Noticing Van Meter's empty arms Coulter inquired why the man had no soap samples with him, Van Meter insisted that the samples were down in his car. When pressed by Coulter to provide some type of identification, Van Meter again stated that everything was down in his car. Not looking to play 20 questions Van Meter quickly descended down the stairs. Detective Coulter was convinced that Van Meter was no ordinary salesman and decided to follow down after him. Once Coulter reached the lobby he discovered that Van Meter had vanished. Turning to head back upstairs Coulter spotted an armed Van Meter hiding behind the basement staircase. Without hesitation Van Meter popped out from the staircase and hollered that he was going to give the lawman exactly what he wanted and then started firing away at Coulter. Agent Coulter grabbed for his gun and returned fire as he fell through the front door out onto the lawn. In an odd reversal of roles Van Meter now gave chase after a fleeing Coulter. The chase continued until the intersection of Lexington and Lincoln at which point Van Meter retreated back into the building.

Meanwhile back at room 303, things were about to turn violent. Looking to shoot his way out of the building Dillinger had opened the apartment door just enough to squeeze out the muzzle of his machine gun. The building echoed as Dillinger littered the hallway with bullets. Once the hallway was clear, Billie and Dillinger casually walked out the building's back door. Dillinger was still carrying his machine gun as Billie ran towards the hidden getaway car that was being stored at a nearby three-car garage. Billie grabbed the car, and after some arguing about her choice of the getaway direction, Dillinger got in and the two sped off toward Minneapolis (See Dr. May's). The *Sheboygan Journal* reported that a trail of blood was found outside the apartment, leading investigators to believe that one of the gangsters had been injured during the battle. The wounded gangster was Dillinger, who had been shot in his left leg and was dripping blood while he made his daring escape out the back door. With Dillinger and Billie gone, Van Meter was on his own to escape. Looking to get out of the area by any means possible, Van Meter showed some creativity and stole a garbage collector's horse and trotted away to safety along Lincoln Avenue. The authorities were originally unsure as to the identities of the gun-fighting men. A search of the apartment uncovered all the essential items that a bank robber would need, including numerous guns, ammunition, a couple of bullet proof vests, and a detailed escape plan from an Iowa bank robbery. The *Emporia Gazette* reported that the authorities had found a newspaper in the abandoned car of the second suspect (Van Meter) which was opened up to a story about Dillinger. This piece of evidence lead the authorities to believe that the injured man was Dillinger. A few hours later their assumptions were confirmed when several personal photos of

Dillinger were discovered inside the apartment. Once again Dillinger and Van Meter had somehow eluded certain capture, a move that only enhanced their already enormous reputations. But how long could their luck continue?

Tommy Gun Adventures:

The Lincoln Court Apartments are still standing and, although the building is on private property, you can still pull your car around the back and make your own getaway route, just like Dillinger did.

Homer Van Meter Gets Gunned Down

Location:

Corner of University and Marion Street

St. Paul, MN 55103

Directions:

Follow University Avenue to Marion Street. The area where Van Meter was killed is just south on Marion, approximately where the University Bank parking lot is.

Gangster Lore:

Although not extremely well-known by today's general public, Homer Van Meter was one of John Dillinger's most trusted friends and colleagues. Having met in prison, the two men set out on one of the greatest crime sprees in U.S. history. Together, with a handful of other deadly gangsters, the two robbed banks, stole from police stations, and even underwent plastic surgery together in order to conceal their identities. It seems only fitting that the pair of men who started out together, and spent much of their time on the run together, would meet their fate in such eerily similar conditions.

History:

1906 – Homer Van Meter was born in Fort Wayne Indiana. He suffered a hard childhood living with an alcoholic father. His turbulent home life forced him to run away with dreams of making it to the big city of Chicago.

1923 – Van Meter's first arrest came from a charge of being drunk and disorderly. Later that same year Van Meter ended up back in jail for committing larceny.

1924 – Van Meter was paroled from jail and wasted no time getting right back into a life of crime, as he joined up with a former cell mate and attempted to rob a passenger train in Indiana. Van Meter was caught once again, this time he was sentenced to 10 to 21 years in Pendleton Reformatory. It was in Pendleton that Van Meter met a fellow inmate named John Dillinger. The two quickly became close friends and often talked of grandiose plans once they were both free.

1925 – Numerous behavior issues forced Van Meter to be transferred to the State Prison in Michigan.

1933 – Having had several failed escape attempts, and frequent additional behavior problems, Van Meter somehow convinced the state clemency commission that he had been reformed. Van Meter was paroled from prison by Governor Paul V. McNutt.

1933 – The very same year as his parole, Van Meter robbed a bank in Michigan with fellow gangsters George "Baby Face" Nelson and Tommy Carroll.

1934 – Van Meter, along with Baby Face Nelson, John Hamilton, Eddie Green, John Dillinger, and Tommy Carroll, robbed a South Dakota bank of over $46,000.

1934 – Van Meter was gunned down in St. Paul.

Investigation:
On August 23, 1934, Homer Van Meter left the St. Paul Motors car dealership and headed for a car that was parked on University Avenue just north of Marion Street. He had no idea of what was about to happen, as he was immediately ambushed by two waiting lawmen (Tom Brown and Frank Cullen). The *Mason City Globe-Gazette* reported that the waiting lawmen, armed with sawed-off shotguns, claimed that they had told Van Meter to "surrender." The *Brainerd Daily Dispatch* claimed that Van Meter "replied with the only language he knew—gunfire," as he fired two shots at the police while he took off running south

along Marion Street. Looking for a quick escape, Van Meter turned left into a small alleyway on Marion Street. Unfortunately for Van Meter, the alley was a dead end, and as soon as he discovered his fatal mistake he was blasted in the back by the lawmen's shotguns. The powerful blast sent Van Meter sprawling to the ground. Like a true gangster, a bloodied Van Meter desperately attempted to grab his gun in order to return fire. The only problem was that his hand and arm had been nearly blown off by the shotgun blast, making it nearly impossible for him to grab onto anything. Within a couple of minutes death had claimed Homer Van Meter in the alleyway, much the same way that Dillinger was gunned down only a month prior.

The police reported that in addition to the 50 bullets in his body, Van Meter also was carrying over $900 in cash and was equipped with a fancy gold pocket watch. In 1934, nine hundred dollars was a large sum of money, but Van Meter's girlfriend claimed that he had over $2,000 in his money belt alone and was carrying a little zipped bag with over $6,000 in it. Witnesses to the shooting also reported that Van Meter was carrying a small bag. The missing money was never officially accounted for. With Homer Van Meter dead, one would assume that his story was over, but actually the real story had just begun.

To put it mildly, the death of Van Meter sparked heavy speculation among the both the press and the underground players. The mysterious events surrounding the death of Van Meter spun numerous competing theories and fostered many unanswered questions. The first question on everybody's mind was how the police came to know that Van Meter would be on University Avenue at that exact time. The *North Adams Transcript* reported that Van Meter "was betrayed unwittingly by his interest in a woman." The main theory was that a relative of one of the women Van Meter was seeing because fearful for her safety. In order to protect this unknown woman he had alerted the authorities to Van Meter's whereabouts. Although the *Logansport Pharos-Tribune* reported that this woman's name was being withheld from the public, it was widely assumed that the woman was Opal Mulligan. One day later, the *St. Paul Daily Dispatch* ran a story that claimed that Opal Mulligan was being held for questioning by the St. Paul Police, which only seemed to confirm her connection. Another more sinister theory of the killing suggests that Van Meter was actually betrayed by one of his own. On August 26,

1934, the *Lincoln Star* ran a *United Press* article that told of Van Meter being "outlawed by his own cronies and betrayed by the underworld." Word was that Van Meter had gone to the Green Lantern Saloon, which at the time was run by underworld banker Harry Sawyer, to collect his share of the $49,000 that the Dillinger gang had robbed from a South Dakota bank. It was said that many of the underworld players of St. Paul were not happy with all of the "heat" Van Meter was bringing to the area. It is assumed that Sawyer thought that by ratting Van Meter out, he could get the FBI off his case, and keep Van Meter's money for himself. The media appeared to collaborate this theory, and on August 26, the *Syracuse Herald* wrote that Van Meter's colleagues were "fearful that his continued presence would bring upon themselves pressure which city, state, and, national authorities have concentrated upon Dillinger's gang, members of the gang decided to betray Van Meter." Even with the hundreds of newspaper articles, internal investigations, witness interviews, and FBI probes, the events leading to the killing of Van Meter have remained a mystery. What happened to the nearly $7,000 that he was carrying when he died is a much easier mystery to solve.

Tommy Gun Adventures:
Although little of what the landscape looked like in the 1930s is still recognizable, and all of the identifying buildings that were there when Van Meter was killed are now gone, you can still go to the general area of his death and check it out. The alley where he was gunned down was approximately where University Av-

enue and the University Bank's parking lot meet. You can follow in Van Meter's footsteps and head south down Marion, cross University Avenue, and head into the bank parking lot. Just be sure you don't tell the bank officials that you are looking for a dead bank robber.

STAPLES
MINNESOTA

The Unsolved Robbery of the First National Bank

Location:

111 4th St. NE

Staples, MN 56479

(218) 894-2943

Currently: First International Bank

Directions:

Follow Highway 10 (2nd Ave NE) to the west into downtown Staples. Turn right onto 4th St. NE and the bank will be in the middle of the block on your left side.

Gangster Lore:

It is not hard to imagine why the gangsters would have targeted the First National Bank in Staples. Only a couple of hours away from the Twin Cities, the bank was rumored to be overflowing with the money from payroll deposits of the local railroad company.

Add in the extremely small police force of the time, and the little city of Staples provided the gangsters with a perfect opportunity to knock off their bank, which of course they did.

History:

1900s – The First National Bank began operations in Staples.

1931 – Five armed bandits robbed the First National Bank of $17,000.

1980s – The First National Bank was gone and the First Integrity Bank operated in the building.

2008 – The bank operating in the building once again changed to the First Integrity Bank. The bank was closed by the Office of the Comptroller of the Currency (OCC) and the Federal Deposit Insurance Corporation (FDIC) was named Receiver. All deposit accounts were transferred over to the First International Bank. The official reason of the bank closing was listed as "unsafe practices had weakened its financial condition."

2008 – The First International Bank took over operations of the bank.

Currently- The building houses the First International Bank and is open to the public.

Investigation:

It was just after 9 a.m. when the first customers of the day began to file into the First National Bank to conduct their daily business. Unbeknownst to them, five armed gangsters waiting nearby had other plans for the bank's money. As the five-man crew made its way toward the bank, the first man stayed back with the getaway car. The second man was positioned inside the bank door, and the remaining three bandits calmly strolled into the bank lobby. In a matter of mere seconds the men had taken control of the entire bank. The *Staples World* wrote that the gunmen first covered the Assistant Cashier (K.R. Johnson) then moved their guns to the Cashier (K.T. Barrett) while the third gunmen entered the office of Mr. Nims. Inside of the office the gangster surprised Mr. Nims, who was engaged in conversation with Police Chief Britton, who was quickly relieved of his weapon. Luckily only two customers were inside the bank at the time of the robbery. The customers and staff were rushed to the rear of the building where they were instructed to get down of the floor, with their faces down. Once the bank was secured, the robbers set about scooping up all the available money they could locate. In order to get to the "big money" the robbers used their guns to "persuade" the vice-president and bank cashier to assist them in opening the vault. A few moments after the heist began, two railroad employees entered the bank and were promptly greeted by the man guarding the front door. The late arrivals were also ushered to the back office where they enjoyed the "comfort" of the hard floor with the others. During the next few minutes a few more stragglers wandered into the bank and were given the same treatment as the others. Among the new hostages was the editor of the newspaper, *Staples World*. The editor took the robbery in stride and added some levity when he later stated that the vice-president's office was so full of people laying face down that it looked like "midnight in a 5-cent flop house." After a few tense moments the hostages noticed that the bank had become eerily quiet. Cashier Barrett slowly crawled out of the office to see what was taking place, and discovered that the gunmen were gone, and so was the bank's money. Immediately, Barrett ran outside in order to sound the alarm and noticed that those outside had been given orders to keep their hands raised until the gunmen were long gone. Amazingly no shots were fired throughout the entire robbery.

Upon swiftly exiting the bank, the robbers hopped in their car and sped off toward Highway 2. A local man who had acquired a high-powered rifle took one shot at the car as the robbers escaped, but the speeding vehicle was already too far away to be damaged. News of the daring morning robbery quickly spread through the area, and soon reports of the speeding getaway car came in from every corner of the county. Unfortunately, none of the sightings were able to lead police to the robbers, and the case has never been solved. So who could have been responsible for this crime? In an odd coincidence, this bank robbery happened exactly one year to the day from the bank robbery in Willmar (see Bank of Willmar). Although no one was ever charged with the robbery, all the witnesses say it was done by professionals who knew what they were doing. The *Staples World* wrote "to say that the crew of bandits were old hands at the game is putting it mild—they were past-masters at their art." The *Bismarck Tribune* ran a quote from Mr. Nims stating that "they worked very cleverly and swiftly. No one ever would have suspected they were robbers as they entered the bank." It is likely that the gunmen chose the date of the 15th with the anticipation that the bank would be flush with money from the Northern Pacific payroll deposits, a belief which ended up being untrue. When all was said and done the gunmen had made off with $14,000 in cash, and an additional $3,000 in travelers checks, both of which were covered by insurance. In an effort to thwart off follow up robberies local residents armed with guns spent the next few months patrolling the bank on payroll day.

I stopped into the First International Bank naively looking to re-live the robbery. As you can probably imagine I received several puzzled looks from the staff as I inquired about the details from the bank robbery of 1931. Much to my dismay not one staff member was aware that their building and bank had been the site of a 1931 bank robbery. My luck took a turn for the better when I entered in the Staples World Newspaper. There I was intro-duced to the paper's editor, Tom Crawford, who had done exten-sive research into the robbery. Not only had Crawford dug through the original newspaper articles, he gone so far as to track down and interview a woman who had been inside the bank dur-ing the robbery. In 1991, Tom wrote an excellent article about his interview with Ruth Walker, who was working as a waitress in Staples during 1931. Normally Ruth's boss had the responsi-bility of depositing the restaurant's daily earnings, but on the day of the robbery he was a bit under the weather and sent Ruth over to the bank instead. During the interview she told Crawford she remembered, "There were five of them; each one had a gun. I was ordered to lie down on the floor." Even after 60 years, she was able to recall certain details of the robbery that were forever engrained into her memory. In a fitting end to the story, when asked if she was proud to be the last person from the bank rob-bery that was still alive, the 94-year-old replied, "Oh, gosh, I don't know."

Tommy Gun Adventures:
If you want to follow the same escape route that the gunmen mapped out, continue down First Ave. until the street ends, circle

around onto Second St. and head back for the freedom of Highway 2. You might want to keep an eye on your tires because when the gangsters reached the highway they threw out handfuls of roofing nails to halt any pursuing vehicles.

STILLWATER
MINNESOTA

Phil's Tara Hideaway

Location:

15021 60th St. N.

Oak Park Heights, MN 55084 (Stillwater)

(651) 439-9850

www.tarahideaway.com

Directions:

From Stillwater head south on Main Street (Highway 36/95); when 96 and 36 split follow highway 36 to the west toward Oak Park Heights. Turn left on Osgood Ave. N. Take an immediate left on 60th St. N (unmarked corner). Follow the road to the dead end where Phil's Tara Hideaway is located.

Gangster Lore:

During Prohibition the "roadside hideaway" played an integral role throughout the United States. These speakeasies were usually constructed directly off of main roads in rural areas just outside of nearby city limits. The strategic placing of the speakeasy ensured that even the smallest of city laws would be stretched in these "hidden" places. This was extremely important when you considered that speakeasies were places where booze, gambling, and ladies of the night could be obtained. This combination of social ills provided the perfect hideout for gangsters looking to lay low when the heat got to be too much.

History:

1920s – The place was operated as an underground speakeasy where many gangsters including Al Capone, John Dillinger, Baby Face Nelson, and the Barker-Karpis gang hung out.

1929 – Gerald "Whitey" Lynch and his brother Eugene established Lynch's Chicken Shack on the property.

1932 – A fire completely destroyed the original building. Lynch decided to re-build the business.

1932 – Within six months of the fire the new business was back in operation. Paying homage to the area's logging history, the new building was constructed entirely of logs. The business was called the Log Cabin, and it is believed that Lynch initially wanted to add fuel pumps on the location due to a contract he signed with an oil company, but no evidence that pumps were ever installed has been found.

1933 – Seeing the end of Prohibition coming, George and his wife, Nettie, arranged for a mortgage of $400 from the Hamm Brewing Company.

1937 – The Log Cabin suffered a break-in that resulted in the loss of both money and supplies.

1938 – The business was sold to Nick Michels. Mr. Michels decided to retain the Log Cabin name.

1946 – The Log Cabin was purchased by Herbert Thiessen who changed the name of the business to Club Tara Hideaway.

1966 – Robert Browning became the new owner of the restaurant and the name of the business was shortened to Club Tara.

1994 – A group of new investors purchased the property intending to run it as a restaurant.

1996 – The business was sold to Ryszard Biernacki. However, legal problems plagued Mr. Biernacki and he was forced to sell the business.

1997 – The current owner, Phil Barbatsis, purchased the property. Once again the name was changed, this time becoming Phil's Tara Hideaway.

2007 – The building was listed on the National Register of Historic Places.

Currently – The restaurant is open to the public.

Investigation:

It has been long rumored that the Log Cabin served as a hot spot for traveling gangsters who were seeking some drinks and entertainment betweens trips from Chicago to St. Paul. At the time the secluded out of town location of the Log Cabin would have provided the gangsters with a perfect amount of privacy from the prying eyes of the authorities. Although many virtually unknown gangsters made the speakeasy their second home, it was the most infamous of these characters that sparked all of the legends. During the 1920s Al Capone was said to have stopped into the speakeasy while he was in the area checking on his Minnesota business. John Dillinger was also thought to have spent many nights enjoying the benefits of the speakeasy. There is also some uncertainty as to when the Chicken Shack was established. Many sources have the Lynch brothers opening it in 1929, while others sources believe the business began in 1931-32. To muddy the matter even more, the Federal Census of 1930 lists George and Nettie Lynch as being residents of Detroit Michigan and not Minnesota. However, the 1930-31 Stillwater City Directory listed George and Nettie as being the proprietors of a restaurant in Oak Park, MN. Although the true beginning date is still being sought, the real importance is not when the speakeasy opened, but just who it opened for.

Local legend also tells of a daring kidnapping in the Stillwater area in which the Log Cabin was ground zero. It is said that many years ago a Stillwater resident kidnapped a liquor salesman possibly for ransom or some unpaid debts. The kidnapped man was said to have been brought to the Log Cabin and kept in the basement during the crime. Older residents of the area even claim that the kidnapper was sent to prison for the crime, but no evidence of this has yet surfaced. The Washington County Historical Society confirmed that the lore of the Log Cabin being a place for gangsters has been whispered throughout the community since the 1920s. Older seniors in the community remember their parents telling them stories of the flashy gangsters that frequented the Log Cabin. However, the historical society was also quick to point out that no substantial proof of the gangster/log cabin ties can be found. I spoke with the current owner who wholeheartedly believed that gangsters had often used the speakeasy as a place to unwind and relax. The restaurant even showcases its gangster past by using John Dillinger in some of their advertising. I guess the only way to reach a conclusion on this case is to venture over to the hideaway and decided its history for yourself. Just in case, be sure to sit with your back to the wall.

Terrorized by Gunfire of Desperadoes

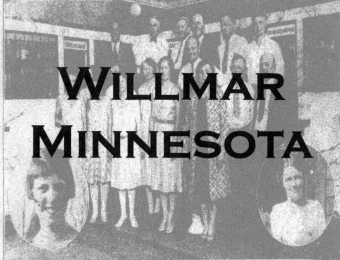

WILLMAR
MINNESOTA

Principal victims in the daring machine-gun holdup of the Bank of Willmar, Tuesday, are shown above after the robbery. In the upper picture are sixteen employes of the bank who were among the 25 victims of the robbery. They are, front row, left to right, Miss June Fladeboe, Miss Alice Reitmann, Miss Laila Nordstrom, Arthur J. Swenson, Adeline Sundberg, Mrs. Agnes Tommeraasen, Miss Eleanor Gordhamer, A. H. Nordstrom, Miss Marie Wackson, a customer, Elnar Brogren and George M. Robbins. Miss Wacker and Mr. Robbins were forced to act as shields for two robbers as they left the bank. In the rear row are Norman H. Tallakson, cashier; C. F. Olson, vice president; A. Straxness, assistant cashier; Ed Selvig, vice president, E. L. Tommeraasen and Howard Hong. In the insets in the upper picture are the two women who were shot down by the robbers outside the bank. At the upper left is Mrs. Thomas Gildia, wounded in the leg and at the right is her mother, Mrs. Emil Johnson, who is believed to be dying. In the lower picture is A. H. Nordstrom, assistant cashier, showing how he touched off a burglar alarm as he lay prone in a teller's cage.

Bank Bandits Active

NAVAL PACT CAUSE ENDS

DRY AGENTS KIDNAPPED

171

The Willmar Bank Gets Robbed

Location:

302 5th Street SW

Willmar, MN 56201

Currently: Christianson & Associates PLLP

Directions:

From Highway 12 (Pacific Ave. SW), turn left on 5th St. SW and follow it. Just as you pass the intersection of Litchfield Ave. SW you will see the old bank building on your right.

Gangster Lore:

The newspapers called the Willmar Bank robbery one of the most daring bank holdups in the Northwest since the days of the

Younger Brothers and Jesse James gangs, which is high praise in the world of crime. When you consider all of the terror the robbery caused, perhaps the praise was warranted.

The robbery turned out to be a very bloody affair, and although several innocent bystanders were severely injured, and at least two of the robbers got shot, the casualties could have been far worse.

History:

1869 – A railroad line was placed through the town of Willmar, which at the time only consisted of a few homes sprinkled throughout the area. With the railroad came an increase in commerce, leading to the creation of a mill, an elevator, and several shops.

1876 – The community need for a bank was recognized by N.H. Corson of Minneapolis, who established the Bank of Willmar.

1877 – After just one year of operation the bank was sold to Mr. A.B. Robbins. Mr. Robbins was a man of some note who was the founder of Robbinsdale, MN. Mr. T.H. Weston severed as a broker in the bank.

1886 – Mr. A.E. Rice served as the president of the bank. Mr. Rice was also a well-respected business leader and political leader in the Willmar community.

1920s – The downturn in agriculture caused a dramatic decline in the bank's profits, forcing the bank to accept financial aid from Mr. Otto Bremer of St. Paul.

1926 – Besides the Bank of Willmar, the city was also home to the First National Bank, the Kandiyohi County Bank, and the Farmers State Bank.

1928 – Due to the increasingly scarce banking business several consolidations took place. The first consolidation began when the Kandiyohi County Bank absorbed the Union Bank.

1929 – The Bank of Willmar absorbed the Kaniyohi County Bank. A few months later the Bank of Willmar took over the First National Bank as well.

1930 – Being the only bank remaining in town, the Bank of Willmar posted deposits of $3,257,000 and loans outstanding of $2,071,000.

1930 – On July 15th the Bank of Willmar was robbed.

1933 – President Franklin D. Roosevelt closed all the banks in the country, and a bank holiday was declared in order for banks to get their finances in order. Drastic changes came to the Bank of Willmar, as the deposits of over 2500 people had been reduced by 50 percent. Mr. Otter Bremer stepped in again and invested over half a million dollars into the Bank of Willmar.

1940-2000s – The Bremer Bank operated in the building.

1996 – As part of the town's 125th Jubilee celebration, a re-en-actment of the 1930 bank robbery was performed.

2006 – The CPA Firm of Christianson & Associates moved into the building.

Source: The Centennial History of Kandiyohi County Minnesota 1870-1970

Investigation:
On the sunny morning of July 15, 1930, five heavily armed and nicely dressed men entered the downtown Bank of Willmar with the intention of robbing it. The time was 10:30 am and the robbers drove up to the bank in their large Buick. One man stayed with the car and another stood lookout in front of the bank, holding a machine gun in his hands. The three remaining robbers entered the bank brandishing revolvers. Immediately the employees were ordered down onto the floor where they were threatened that if anyone so much as moved, they would be killed. The *Willmar Tribune* reported that when Ernest Person lifted his head from the ground and asked if he should keep his head down, the gunman replied, "Damn you, yes, or I'll fill you with lead." The robbers first targeted the teller cage of employee A.E. Nordstrom and cleaned out $9,000 before scooping up another $9,000 from George Robbins' cage. Risking certain death if caught, two separate employees sounded the alarm, and while all the terror was

unfolding inside the bank, a large crowd of curious residents began to form outside the bank. The bandits hurried into the bank vault where they removed over $55,000 in currency along with another $40-$50 thousand in negotiable bonds.

Outside the bank, three local men (Sam Evens, "Jolly" Peterson, and R.S. Paffrath) heeded the bank's alarm and quickly gathered up some guns and rushed toward the bank while firing several shots at the getaway driver, which prompted the man covering the front door to unload a barrage of machine gun fire in return. Hearing the gunfire exploding outside, the robbers gathered up several employees to use as human shields as they exited the bank. Once outside, the group encountered more gunfire and re-turn shots were blasted. During the mayhem, the getaway driver was struck with a bullet and witnesses saw his body slump over in the seat. As the robbers sprayed the area with gun fire, two women (Mrs. Emil Johnson and Mrs. D. Gildea) were struck by the bullets, luckily they both would survive. The *St. Paul Pioneer Press* wrote that it was a "miracle that a dozen by-standers were not killed."   Safe from the onslaught of gunfire the robbers ditched their human shields and tore off down 5th St. toward the Village of Kandiyohi. Along the way they

tossed handfuls of tacks onto the gravel road to help halt any attempts at pursuit. The bank robbery was never officially solved, but General Rhinow told the *Willmar Tribune* that "These bandits were professionals without question." It is now believed that the five bandits were: Sammy Silverman, George "Machine Gun" Kelly, Robert Steinhardt, Harvey Bailey, and Verne Miller. The newspapers had been right in their assumptions about the men being professionals, and considering the gang's loose trigger fingers perhaps it was a miracle that many more bystanders were not killed.

Tommy Gun Adventures:
I was able to get a tour of the original bank vault from the 1930 robbery. The vault is located in the basement of the building and it requires special permission to gain access, so be sure to brush up on your manners and persuasion skills.

WYOMING
MINNESOTA

The Ransom Payment and Release of William Hamm

Location:

Former farm

Wyoming, MN 55092

Directions:

There are several locations tied to the ransom payment and release of William Hamm. Here are a few of the more prominent public locations:

Ransom Money Drop – Pine City, MN
William Dunn dropped off the $100,000 ransom payment some-
where along Highway 61 between Rush City and Pine City. The
stretch of road between the two cities is approximately 12 miles.

William Hamm Released – Wyoming, MN
Most newspapers reported that Hamm was released on a deserted
highway in Wyoming Minnesota. It is assumed that he was released near Highway 61. However a few newspapers reported
that after being released Hamm stumbled to the farm of Mrs.
Anna Verges. Old records show that the Verges family did own a
chunk of land located on the southeast corner of 260th Street and
Goodview Avenue in Wyoming, right across the street from
Goodview Park. This was the farm where Hamm used the phone
to call his family in St. Paul. Whether by complete coincidence,
or as a final ironic joke played by the gang, the farm just north of
where William Hamm was dropped off was owned by a man
named Conrad Hamm.

Rosedale Pharmacy – (Now Thomas Liquors)

1941 Grand Avenue, St. Paul.

Fred Goetz wandered into the store and purchased a couple of items while leaving a ransom note to be delivered to Mr. Dunn. You can still see a photo of the original pharmacy at the main entrance of the store.

Gangster Lore:

When dealing with the volatile Barker-Karpis gang, you really had no idea of what would transpire. Put yourself in the unfortunate position of William Hamm. He was a 39-year-old millionaire businessman that had just been kidnapped by a group of unsavory men and brought to an undisclosed location. Hamm was bright young man and had to have immediately realized that these men were certainly not to be fooled with. Although they treated him very well, he could have only wondered what they ultimately had in store for him. Negative thoughts certainly flowed through his head, as he could only wait and hope that things would miraculously play out in his favor. Perhaps it was best for Hamm's sanity that he had no real idea just how dangerous the men behind his kidnapping were.

History:

1933 – While leaving work for lunch William Hamm was abducted by the Barker-Karpis gang. Hamm was held captive in Illinois while the gangsters negotiated a $100,000 ransom payment.

1933 – After receiving the ransom payment, the Barker-Karpis gang dropped Hamm off in Wyoming, MN where he called home and let his family know he was okay.

Investigation:

With the actual kidnapping of William Hamm, the gang had completed the easy part of their plan. The hard part would be securing the $100,000 ransom payment they were seeking. In order to accomplish their goal the gang needed Hamm's assistance. The first step was to ask Hamm, who among his friends and family would make the best contact person for the important ransom negotiations. Hamm thought for a minute, and then gave the name of William Dunn, who severed as the brewery's sales manager. At 5 p.m. Dunn received a call from an unknown man. The caller informed him that they had kidnapped Hamm, and that they were seeking a $100,000 ransom for his safe return. The caller demanded that the money be paid in twenties, tens, and fives, and that Dunn would hear from them later. The caller then provided detailed instructions on the ransom process. After receiving the message, Dunn called the St. Paul Police. Immediately the FBI placed wiretaps on Dunn's phone in hopes of tracking down the kidnappers. A few hours later, Dunn received another call from the gang and was told that the gangsters had given him time to recover from the news of the earlier call, and assured him that all he had to do was follow their orders and Hamm would be returned safely. According to the *Mason City Globe-Gazette*, on June 16, an unknown man (Fred Goetz) paid a taxi driver two dollars to deliver a note to William Dunn. The note stated that the family was to pay off the $100,000, and if they failed to comply with demands, they would never see Hamm again. The newspaper also reported that the taxi driver positively identified a photograph of Verne Sankey. This witness identification, along with other evidence gathered led police down the wrong path to Sankey. The June 17, edition of the *St. Paul Pioneer Press* reported that the police believed Verne Sankey, who had also kidnapped a young man just a year prior to the Hamm kidnapping, had organized Hamm's kidnapping.

The next day Fred Goetz walked into the Rosedale Pharmacy and purchased a couple of small items. After making his purchase, Goetz left the pharmacy. A few moments after he left, the pharmacy received an unusual call. The unidentified caller directed the clerk to a ransom note that Goetz had placed in the store to be delivered to Dunn's nearby home. This ransom note took a darker tone than the previous one, with the gang cussing out Dunn and warning him that there would be consequences for any attempt at double-crossing them. The next day another note was left for Dunn in the back seat of a Hamm's Brewing employee's car. This note contained detailed instructions on how the ransom payment would be handled. Dunn was instructed to travel along Highway 61 and to keep his eye out for five flashes of a car's headlights, which would serve as a signal for Dunn to drop the money on the road. The note also stated that Mr. Hamm was very disappointed with the manner in which Dunn had handled this case so far. Wanting to secure the safe return of Hamm, Dunn retrieved the ransom money and headed north on Highway 61.

When Dunn was near Pine City, he spotted the signal and dropped the briefcase full of the ransom money. As soon as the briefcase was dropped, a car with Fred Barker, Fred Goetz, and Charles Fitzgerald pulled over and scooped up the money. Dunn drove up to Duluth and checked into the Hotel Duluth to await further instructions.

Once the money had been retrieved and inspected, the gang got ready for the release of their captive. Hamm was given a new set of clothes and fed a final meal. The *Jefferson City Post-Tribune* included Hamm's account of the release: "That night, Sunday, we started out after dark, two men, the driver, and myself. They put the goggles back on me and after another ride they left me out at Wyoming on the main highway.

I had some money. They made no effort to take it from me while I was a prisoner. They didn't say anything after letting me go and it was kind of dark so I couldn't see what kind of car was used." After being set free, Hamm staggered to the farm of Mrs. Anna Verges and asked to use her phone. The *Fresno Bee Republican* reported that Mrs. Verges asked Hamm where he wanted to go, but he told her "that he didn't know where he wanted to go because he didn't know where he was." Hamm then placed a call to his home in St. Paul to notify his family that he was free. According to the *Chester Times*, Mr. Dunn was in Duluth with Inspector Charles Tierney, waiting for the news of Hamm's release. When the call came in that Hamm had been released, the two men sped off south to pick him up near Wyoming. Hamm was brought to his home in St. Paul while the gangsters excitedly counted their money and plotted even bigger kidnappings.

ONGRESSMEN CLASH WITH FCA HEAD ON CREDIT

ederal Aid Banks Business Institutions, Myers Tells Midwest Solons

Washington, Feb. 1 — Many idwestern congressmen do not see ye-to-eye with the farm credit administration the jumping off place itween credit and charity.

That, plus political complications be expected in a bankint business sembling the postoffice department in magnitude, has in it the akings of a headache for Dr. William L. Myers, a former college professor who less than four months go became governor of the farm edit administration.

Recently, Myers, known as "Bill" young executives of the FCA, sat rough a hearing of the house rules mmittee during consideration of e investigation resolution ard the FCA called "bureaucra ," "the land banks criticized iggardily" land appraisals, harges that republicans were ne all the jobs as appraisers.

Leaning across his desk later, My-ers told an interviewer he and his ssistants were straining themselves o do the best they could to perform big job.

"Every single complaint on our ir appraisals is checked," he said.

The land banks are but one of the ations. Myers said, and his chief ook barons assigned as of the big ad mortgage man from foreclosing h farms. Only outright charity ould save a good many, he said.

Hollywood Sights

—By ROBBIN COONS—

Hollywood — Embodying enough yphsally winsome Janet Gaynor footage" to be appealing to her ans, "Carolina" at the same time makes a bid for the consideration of hose who like more solid dramatic ood.

The new film, co-starring Janet with Lionel Barrymore, is an adaptation of Paul Green's play, "The House o' Connelly." It is the story of the charge wrought in an aristocratic but indigent southern family y the advent of a little Pennsylvania girl with new ideas.

The Connellys, portrayed variously by Henrietta Crosman, Barrymore and Robert Young, live in poverty and pride on their dilapidated plantation, feeding on memories of the grandeur they knew before the Civil war, but having difficulty with the charge account at the country tore. The son (Young) is restless, but indifferent.

A Yankee Invasion

Come Janet as daughter of a tenant farmer on the place. When he dies, Janet carries on, raising her tobacco crop, although Mrs. Connelly a positive the soil won't grow to-bacco—and this being about 1900, the Carolina tobacco industry hasn't risen to prove her wrong. Janet, wn are to infer, is a pioneer.

Place of Bremer Release Here Not Yet Determined

Authorities Refuse to Admit Investigation Is Being Conducted Here

Continued uncertainty as to the spot where Edward G. Bremer, kidnaped St. Paul banker, was released ad here was announced by Rochester police today.

The location of the hideout to which he was taken by the kidnap gang January 17 also remained uncertain, although apparently it was a considerable distance from Rochester as Bremer said in St. Paul that he remembered being placed in a car with three other men and being driven several hours prior to his release.

Bremer was released shortly before 8 p.m. Wednesday, but the development was not learned of here until yesterday morning. He went to his home after taking a train from here to Owatonna and a bus from that city to St. Paul.

Released in City

fact that Bremer was ... Rochester ... eratives continued their search for the abductors today and several ef-les were reported to be scenes of investigations. Operatives at St. ... refused to admit that agents ... ... investigation ... ... turned to St. Paul after conferring with Chief Claude.

An informal report that Bremer believed he was released shortly after passing over a bridge and that he passed a woodlot soon after his release caused some belief it might have been on South Broadway near the business district. This is not a residential area. Two other highways, 55 and 50, pass over bridges near the city, it was pointed out.

Chief Claude and the justice department operative investigated roads leading into the city but failed to find any trace of the scene of the release. Police were reported to have sought goggles and bandages worn by Bremer, who understood to have said he th... them away.

In ... House

The c... te operative also investigated a house near old Highway 7 east of the city limits and north of the Green Lantern cafe because of rumors that it might have been used as a hideout. The investigation was fruitless.

A rumor that Bremer was held by the kidnapers in Sioux City, Iowa, was denied by federal agents and authorities of that city. The Sioux City angle was reported in St.

Paul to have ... been eliminated as a possibility.

Although Bremer was told by the kidnapers to keep his eyes covered by bandages for five minutes after they released him, he pulled off his bandages and started after their disappearing car. He caught a glimpse of a battered sedan and three occupants. This recalled the report to police here that Douglas Street of Rochester saw a sedan with three men at Lewiston on Highway 14 early yesterday. The car, which displayed New York license plates, was in poor condition.

AGENT WILL SURVEY EMPLOYMENT IN CITY

Mayor and Park Board President Confer With State CWA Engineer

At a conference with Mayor Julius J. Reiter and Art Nachreiner, park board president, in St. Paul, L. F. Zimmerman, state CWA engineer, said he would send Mr. Matters, who ... ... a public meeting ... ... with ... ...berg,

Their return was followed by announcement of plans for a change in CWA methods of employment and for a survey by Mr. Matters to determine unemployment conditions in the city and rural districts separately. Considering also will be given en to condition of unemployed skilled workmen, it was said.

Plans for construction of a headquarters for state highway patrolmen in Rochester were approved by the highway department yesterday, according to an announcement. The project will be carried out by force account and the estimated cost is $5,000.

Appointment of a new state federal re-employment director to succeed O. D. Hollenbeck, who has been promoted to an executive position at Washington, was announced. He is Dreng Bjornaa.

Mr. Hollenbeck sent a letter to Adrian L. Mitten, chairman of the federal re-employment committee for the county, thanking the group for its work. One of the reasons the federal re-employment program got under way so fully was the cooperation given by the various county committees, said Mr. Hollenbeck, who praised Mr. Mitten's work. He urged that similar support be given the new director.

Aided Bremer

Mrs. Jeane Haight, Rochester bus depot attendant, who talked with Edward Bremer shortly after his release by kidnapers here Wednesday night. Through the night's efforts Bremer ... to catch a North West... for Owatonna.

PWA Project Auditor Starts Work in City

P. L. Granquist, federal public ... istration project audi ... to audit records of ... chester, City Clerk A. ... today.

Mr. ... who works out of Minnesota, has been assigned to Minnesota, with headquarters in St. Paul. He will be here at intervals while PWA projects, including construction of two bridges and installation of two units of the trunkline sewer, here in progress.

The bridge projects, in Fourth street SE over the Zumbro river and at Fourteenth street NW over Cascade creek, are in progress and the sewer project will be begun soon.

Pavlova Relics Exhibited

Paris — An exhibition of the art of Anna Pavlova, organized by the Archives Internationale del a Danse, has been opened here to the public. The entire display has been consecrated to the memory of the famous dancer and includes many mementos of her life and art, among which are costumes, portraits, a reconstruction of her room, and a portrayal of her in "The Dying Swan."

Centenarian Rewarded

Ajaccio, Corsica, — Jacques Quilichini, 99 years old, who lives with his two sons, 68 and 64, respectively, in the hamlet of Plano, near Bartene, has been made a knight in the Legion of Honor in recognition of his war record. He fought for France in 1851 and 1859, being wounded at the Battle of Magenta.

THE APPLE CART
10 THIRD ST S.W.   TELEPHONE 1044
ORANGE WEEK
Several hundred pecks of this Health Giving

oranges
florida's juice oranges

ZUMBROTA MINNESOTA

186

The Ransom Payment for Edward Bremer

Location:
Just off Highway 52
Zumbrota, MN 55992

Directions:
The exact location where the ransom payment took place is not known. Your best bet is to travel to Zumbrota along Highway 52. Head south out of town on Highway 52 for about three or four miles, make a left turn when possible, and search for a hill. Here in the middle of nowhere you will be in the general vicinity of where the Bremer family quickly became $200,000 poorer.

Gangster Lore:

After kidnapping William Hamm, the Barker-Karpis gang collected a reported ransom of $100,000. The kidnapping had generated an obscene amount of publicity and pressure for the gang, and for their fellow outlaws. The gang could have easily taken the $100,000 ransom and returned to the simplicity of robbing banks. However, two things would force the gang to press their luck with another kidnapping—money and fame. The prospect of another, ever more lucrative kidnapping, along with the ensuing notoriety from the public, and their colleagues, was simply too tempting for the gang to pass up. As the gang set out to collect the $200,000 ransom for Edward Bremer, they had no idea what it would ultimately cost them.

History:

1933 – The Barker-Karpis gang successfully kidnapped William Hamm. The gangsters ended up receiving a ransom of $100,000 from the Hamm family. Once the ransom payment was made, William Hamm was released without harm.

1934 – The Barker-Karpis gang kidnapped bank president Edward Bremer while he was on his morning drive to work. Bremer was the son of Adolph Bremer, who headed the Jacob Schmidt Brewery Company. Bremer was also the nephew of Otto Bremer, who was a prominent banker and business man with political connections that reached the White House.

1934 – After paying the $200,000 ransom, Edward Bremer was
released by the Barker-Karpis gang in Rochester.

Investigation:

The FBI files on the Barker-Karpis gang give great detail into the
time-line of the Edward Bremer kidnapping and ransom demands. On January 17, the Barker-Karpis gang kidnapped Bremer shortly after he had dropped off his daughter at her school.
While Bremer was being transported to Illinois, where he would
be held captive, the gang proceeded with their ransom plan. At
approximately 10:40 a.m. on January 17, Walter Magee, who
was a close friend of the Bremer family, was working in his office when he received an unnerving call. The unknown man on
the other end of the line informed Magee that his friend Bremer
was being held in their possession. Magee was told that if he
looked out in his yard he would find a note. Magee followed the
instructions and immediately walked over to the side of the
building and found a note lying under a side door. The note had
been addressed to Chas. Magee and read as follows:

> "You are hereby declared in on a very desperate under
> taking. Dont try to cross us. Your future and B's are the
> important issue. Follow these instructions to the letter.
> Police have never helped in such a spot and wont this
> time either. You better take care of the payoff first and let
> them do the detecting later. Because the police usually
> butt in your friend isnt none to comfortable now so dont
> delay the payment. We demand $200,000. Payment must

be made in 5 and 10-dollar bills—no new money—no consecutive numbers—large variety of issues. Place the money in two large suit box cartons big enough to hold the full amount and tie with heavy cord. No contact will be made until you notify us that you are ready to pay as we direct. You place an ad in the *Minneapolis Tribune* as soon as you have the money ready. Under personal col umn (We are ready Alice). You will then receive you final instructions. Be prepared to leave at a minutes no tice to make the payoff. Dont attempt to stall or out smart us. Dont try to bargain. Dont plead poverty we know how much they have in their banks. Dont try to communecate with us we'll do the directing. Threats arent necessary—you just do your part—we guarantee to do ours."

The gang also wanted to put pressure on Magee to get the money as quickly as possible and did this by insinuating that if anything happened to Bremer, it would be Magee's fault. To help with this plan the gang included this handwritten letter from Bremer that read:

"Mr. Chas Magee

I have named you as payoff man. You are responsible for my safety. I am responsible for the full amount of the money.

(Signed) E.G. Bremer

Deal only when signature is used."

Immediately the alarmed Magee contacted the St. Paul Field Division of the Federal Bureau of Investigation, United States Department of Justice, and the St. Paul Police Department to inform them of the kidnapping. The *Wisconsin State Journal* reported "Police were notified, but requested not to enter actively into the case at the request of the family." By this time the authorities had discovered that Bremer's car had been abandoned on Edgecumbe Road in St. Paul. The investigators assumed a struggle had taken place inside the car due to the bloodstains found on the steering wheel, the gear shaft lever, and on the seats. After receiving the news that the bloody automobile was found, several of Bremer's family members feared that Edward was already dead. On January 20, the gang initiated a follow-up contact. Knowing that the authorities were now involved with the case, the gang was forced to contact someone else to deliver a message to Magee. The man they chose was Dr. Henry Nippert. While Nippert was sound asleep, he was briefly awakened by the noise of a crash. Having no idea that a bottle had been thrown through his window, the doctor simply drifted off back to sleep. Moments later Nippert was awoken by a telephone call instructing him to go to the vestibule of his house to see what he could find. Nippert had no problem locating the thrown bottle, and soon found the attached envelope that was addressed to him. Inside the envelope he discovered two additional envelopes addressed to Mrs. Edward Bremer and to Walter Magee. Nippert promptly delivered both the envelopes to Adolph Bremer. The letter that was addressed to Mr. Magee read as follows:

"You must be proud of yourself by now. If Bremer dont get back his family has you to thank. Youve made it al most impossible but were going to give you one more chance—the last. First of all the coppers must be pulled off. Second the dough must be ready. Third we must have a new signal. When you are ready to meet our terms place a N.R.A. sticker in the center of each of your office windows. Well know if the coppers are pulled or not. Remain in your office daily from noon until 8 p.m. Have the dough ready and where you can get it within thirty minutes. You will be instructed how to deliver it. The money must not be hot as it will be examined before Bremer is released. If Dahill is so hot to meet us you can send him out with the dough. Well try to be ready for any trickery if atempted. This is positively out last atempt. DONT duck it."

On January 25, the gang reached out to Magee once again. This time they chose to contact Mr. John Miller. Sometime between 6 and 7 p.m. Miller received a phone call telling him to go home where he would find a Hill Brothers coffee can on his front porch. Upon his arrival home, Miller discovered that his wife had already located the can. The note was addressed to Mr. Magee or Adolph Bremer and instructed that $200,000 must be delivered that evening. The instruction told that the tag, which was enclosed with the note, should be taken to the Jefferson Lines Bus Station. The tag was for a baggage locker in the waiting room of the station, which would contain a bag with further instructions. Mr. Magee was also instructed that this locker hand-bag should not be opened one minute before 8:20 p.m. Mr. Magee heeded the advice of the gangsters and proceeded to the bus depot where he found a black slipper bag which contained a pillow and an additional note. The new note instructed Mr. Magee to assume the name of John B. Brekesham and board a bus leaving St. Paul to Des Moines, Iowa. Meanwhile, the gangsters sent out a note along the route for Magee stating that the ransom plan was off. However, due to the confusion of the plan and the fake name, the note did not reach Magee and the ransom payment fell apart. The gang's well thought out ransom plan was slowly going awry. Each time the gang wrote and delivered these ransom notes the chances of making mistakes increased. Yet at this point the gang clearly needed to re-establish control of the situation and was forced to send out another note. On February 5, somewhere between 7:30 and 8 p.m., an unknown man approached the home of Miss Lillian Dickman. Dickman worked as Bremer's secretary. Dickman encountered the stranger at her back door. The man inquired if she was indeed Lillian Dickman. When she affirmed that she was, the man handed her a note, told her to take care of it, and then left. The note was in Bremer's handwriting and was made out to Adolph Bremer. The note contained an important message that the ransom proceed in accordance with instructions outlined by the gang.

The next day, with their control re-established, the gang sent out yet another message. At approximately 5 p.m., Father Deere was resting at home when an unknown man approached him. The man asked Deere if he was acquainted with a family by the name of Bremer. As soon as Deere confirmed the he knew the family the visitor thrust an envelope into his hand. The envelope was addressed to Chas. Magee or Honest Adolph. Inside the envelope the gangsters explained that the coppers jammed the last payoff, and that if the money was not paid on this night the ransom demand would be increased to $500,000. On the evening of February 6, in compliance with the gangsters' instructions, Magee obtained a Ford sedan. Then, with the $200,000 in ransom money in his possession, he drove in a circuitous route to 969 University Avenue in St. Paul. Once there Magee found a parked 1933 Chevrolet coupe decorated in Shell Oil Company signs. Magee transferred the money from his Ford to the new Chevy. In the left front door pocket he found the keys to the Chevy along with a note that contained these instructions:

"Go to Farmington Minnesota. The Rochester bus will arrive there at 9:15 P.M. Follow one hundred yards in back of this bus, when it leaves Farmington turn on the first road to the left and proceed at fifteen miles per hour until you see five flashes of lights; then stop and deposit packages of money on right hand side of road. Leave the two notes; get in your car and go straight ahead."

Magee followed the instructions and drove off for Farmington. From there Magee followed the bus to Cannon Falls, and then on to Zumbrota. From Zumbrota Magee drove four or five miles until he spotted the four red lights on the left side of the road.

Magee recalled that the lights were positioned on the back of a hill. When Magee came to this point he located a gravel road nearby that lead off to the left. He proceeded down the road slowly, and after covering about half of a mile, a car pulled up behind him and he saw the headlights of the car flash five times. Magee then stopped his Chevy, walked to the rear of the car and grabbed two suit boxes from the right side of the car. He then placed the boxes on the right side of the road, got back in his car, and kept driving forward. In a fitting reversal of roles, Magee was now the one leaving notes as he delivered a letter from Adolph Bremer that read:

> "To parties holding Edward: I've done my part and kept my word 100 percent just as I said I would. This money is not marked and is the full amount asked for. And now, boys I am counting on your honor. Be sports and do the square thing by turning Edward loose at once.
>   (Signed) Adolph Bremer"

Once the ransom was paid, Edward Bremer was released the following day in Rochester. Once Bremer was safe at home the authorities were free to investigate the case with more vigor. On February 8, special agents retraced the route that Magee had taken to pay the ransom money. At a location several miles south of Zumbrota the agents found four flashlights all with a red lens. These lights were tracked back to the F. & W. Grand Silver Store in St. Paul, where a young clerk identified a photograph of Alvin Karpis as being the man who purchased the equipment prior to the kidnapping of Bremer. The gang's luck soured even more when a farmer near Portage, Wisconsin discovered some gasoline cans used for the transport of Bremer. The authorities were able to lift a latent fingerprint from the cans that was identified as being identical with the right index finger of Doc Barker. With the help of Bremer the authorities were even able to locate the home where Bremer was held captive. While the evidence was mounting against the gang, the public and political pressure continued to mount against the act of kidnapping, and it signaled that the end was near for the Barker-Karpis gang...soon they would all be dead or captured.

Tommy Gun Adventures:
You can still retrace the route taken by Walter Magee as he drove out to payoff the Barker-Karpis gang's ransom demands. From St. Paul, head south to Farmington. From here cut west over to Highway 52 and follow it south to Cannon Falls. From Cannon Falls follow the highway to the town of Zumbrota. Once there you can travel a couple of miles south out of town and head left to the general area where the ransom was paid. Just make sure you don't try any funny business along the way.

Comming Soon!

THE WISCONSIN ROAD GUIDE
TO GANGSTER HOT SPOTS

Find out more about this book, upcoming books, authors, blogs,
and more content then we could fit into this printing at:
www.OnTheRoadPublications.com

BIO

Chad Lewis – Is a researcher, author, and lecturer, on top-
ics of the strange and unusual. He has a Master of Science
degree in Psychology and has traveled the globe in search
of unique and bizarre stories and history.   Chad's research
has been featured on numerous national TV shows, radio
interviews, magazines, and newspaper articles. Chad is the
co-author of the Haunted Road Guide series and the author
of the Hidden Headlines series.